Advanced Placement (AP) Adulting

How to Manage Money,

Develop A Mindset for Success, and Navigate

Important Topics Not Taught in School

Cornerstone
Global Media
FOUNDATIONAL EDUCATION

Publisher's Note

Cornerstone
Global Media
FOUNDATIONAL EDUCATION

Distributed by Cornerstone Global Media, LLC.
Copyright © 2022   by Cornerstone Global Media, LLC.
P.O. Box 171
New York, NY 10272

Developmental Editing, Copy Editing and
Proofreading provided by: Lisa Howard
Cover and interior design by: Rafael Andres
Illustrations designed by: Natalia Junqueira

Library of Congress Cataloging-in-Publication Data
Name(s): John Chadwick, Author
Title: Advanced Placement Adulting (AP)
Subtitle: How to Manage Money, Develop a Mindset for Success & Navigate Important Topics Not Taught in School
Identifiers: LCCN Registration Number: TXu 2-298-873;
ISBN 979-8-9857220-5-5
Subject: Self Development; Young Adult Self Improvement; Financial Literacy
US Copyright Type of Case: Literary Work
Registration Decision Date: February 4th, 2022
Publisher: Cornerstone Global Media (a Florida LLC)

Digital Footprint

Visit Us:

www.apadulting.com

Contact Us:

info@apadulting.com

Contents

IN CONCLUSION

CALL TO ACTION

The definition: **AP ADULTING** [uh-dult-ing] – noun – the practice of behaving or acting in a way characteristic of how society defines being a responsible adult, especially the accomplishment of complex and tedious yet necessary tasks and skills needed to achieve what's broadly viewed as adult "success" in life.

Introduction

This is an Advanced Placement course on adulting, a.k.a. accomplishing the complex, tedious, yet necessary tasks needed to achieve what's broadly viewed as adult "success" in life. We're going to get detailed and address concepts that many adults lack knowledge of, particularly young adults. Essentially, this book is for those who want a no-nonsense guide to understanding important concepts that aren't taught in school.

The skills and lessons we learn in school are foundational— we all need to have that background to either continue our formal education or enter the workforce. But after graduating, most people lack practical skills related to finance and personal development for a simple reason: such skills are typically not included in formal classes. Sometimes called "soft skills," they include how to develop a brand at work and how to build generational wealth over time. In this book, along with those topics, we're going to talk about important concepts, like how to manage our personal finances with the goal of developing wealth and how to develop a mindset that best positions us for success. We'll spend some time discussing practical adulting concepts like how taxes work and how to sell and negotiate, too. With these skills in place, you'll have a clear blueprint for achieving adult success.

I wrote this book with my younger self in mind. I really wish I could have understood these concepts 30 years ago. The topics we'll cover won't make the hard work easier, but they will arm you with many of the facts of life that often aren't understood until you actually experience and learn them firsthand. (And find out that the results are often not what you originally expected.) I've learned these concepts through my own experiences, failures, and mistakes, and I hope that reading this book will lessen your learning curve compared to what I went through.

Some of the concepts will be new to you; some will sound familiar. What's important is that you have a clear and open mind and don't get hung up on any one individual concept. The pieces will come together over the course of the book—by the time you've finished it, you will have developed a framework that will enable you to deploy these principles throughout your life. You'll be more confident personally *and* professionally because you'll have references to draw upon when you find yourself in challenging situations or when you need to step back and strategically plan your future. Set your goals high, though. The mistake most people make isn't setting their goals too high and missing them—most people set their goals too low and hit them.

When I graduated from college, I didn't know what I was doing. Maybe that's the case for you, too. That's okay—it goes along with having a lifetime of choices in front of you. You feel like you're ready to take on the world, but you might not know what you don't know. It can take people 10, 20, even 30 years to slowly identify the gaps in their understanding. My hope is that this book will provide a framework for thinking about your choices and your future.

Once you know how some of the financial aspects of life work, you'll be able to deploy your knowledge throughout your life. And when you learn such concepts early on, you'll have much more time to actually utilize these strategies! People who spend their lives learning these lessons are severely disadvantaged because they lose one of the most important factors that lead to success: time in the game. By that, I mean time in the stock market or real estate market, in a career, or even time thinking through who you want to be in 10 years. *What you do right now will result in who you will be in the future.* I want you to be armed with the basics of success. I want you to have the mindset you need to live your desired lifestyle.

Successful people are individuals who set up goals, establish a plan to achieve those goals, and then act against the very next step that's required to reach their goal. Rightly or wrongly, financial success is typically the measure that most people use to define "success." A successful person, though, is really anybody who sets out to achieve a goal and accomplishes it. Financial success happens to be a way to make achieving non-financial goals/successes just a little bit easier. While financial success doesn't necessarily solve all your problems, it does give you one thing: options. And having options allows you to solve many challenges and seize many opportunities.

You may find parts of this book to be more interesting than others. Unfortunately, many people don't find personal finance interesting...and that's why they struggle with money. But personal finance is so important to understand! Understanding it, in many instances, is a prerequisite for having opportunities in your life. Money provides options, and options often open doors and help to solve a number of life's problems.

Commit to your future by committing to reading this book completely. You will pick up on new concepts and ideas in every section, and you'll ultimately have a foundational understanding of many essential financial and mindset principles.

I've broken the content into three broad themes:

1. How to manage and optimize your **personal finances** to build lasting wealth. This will be way more interesting than just putting together a budget—we will learn foundational concepts that will greatly improve our chances of being financially secure in life. Provided, that is, we take the time to learn and implement the principles.
2. How to develop a **mindset for success** that will help frame many of life's decisions and crossroads. We'll talk about how we need to think about opportunities in our life, and we will explore mental tools that will greatly improve our chances of achieving whatever we define as "success."

3. Important concepts that every adult should understand in order to effectively master the art of **AP Adulting.** This is where we'll delve into specific topics that will put us at a real advantage: how to sell, how money works, how stocks work, and how to optimize our time at work, to name a few.

Personal finance is a topic that nearly every self-made, financially successful person has mastered. It's the key to building wealth and not having money problems be a lifetime burden. To that end, we'll cover important topics like how to develop a personal income statement and balance sheet. We'll talk about how to think about consumerism and how people get trapped in the cycle of debt, and we'll walk through the various options we have to build and develop wealth over time. We'll focus on wealth-building tools we already have at our disposal. Many people don't really understand these or don't know enough to choose and prioritize optimal tools. We simply *need* to understand how these tools work at a high level and then commit to taking advantage of them.

We'll also discuss important topics like how stocks work, how we can achieve our goals in retirement, and how we can enjoy financial independence. Even though that last one—financial independence—is easy to understand, it remains a mystery to many people. I love teaching people about being financially independent because it really is life-changing yet attainable for most people.

The section of the book covering the **mindset for success** is more subjective, but it's important to understand the psychological ramifications of different mindsets if we want the best chance of living our desired lifestyle. This section will allow us to think differently about what we perceive as being valuable and quickly get our mindset and energy on a different wavelength. This will put us in a position to have expansive rather than narrowed thinking.

The last section is where we'll get tactical and discuss key **AP Adulting** subject matter that is designed to provide us with a well-rounded understanding of topics that will become more and more relevant in our lives. The content has been specifically identified as subjects that most graduating from formal learning simply haven't been exposed to. Basic topics like how our money system works or how taxes work are everyday concepts that have a big impact on our lives, yet few really understand the mechanics of how they work.

We'll also cover subjects that will have lifelong benefits if understood and used. Topics like optimizing our career and living a healthy lifestyle might seem basic, but, again, many new graduates will go through life and pick up on these subjects by trial and error. After reading the AP Adulting section, you'll have the foundational knowledge that puts you well ahead of your peers. The chapters are indeed Advance Placement, so take the time to read and possibly re-read the heavy content sections. Understanding these topics will allow us to have a well-rounded base that we can build upon over time.

Personal Finance

The topic of personal finance covers a lot of ground. We'll address various aspects related to our budget, our savings rate, and our plan to build long-term wealth.

Personal finance concepts and commercial finance concepts are actually similar. The fundamental metrics that companies look at—like income and expenses—are also applicable to us as individuals. So many of us generate income in the gig economy or through side hustles. Understanding these fundamentals is critical because, in many instances these days, you yourself *are* the actual business. You might be driving for a ride-share app, or you might be employed at a 9-to-5 job. The lines between work and life are becoming more and more blurred, but at the end of the day, whether you're an individual or a large company, it's all about income (revenue) and costs (expenses). The fundamentals of being a financially successful individual and running a financially successful company are the same.

Businesses use basic metrics to ensure they are able to stay open and profitable. Poorly managed businesses run up debt and lose money each month. If left in that state, such a business will eventually close its doors. Successful businesses use metrics to track the cash that comes into the business and cash that leaves the business, and they also keep track of the accumulation of assets (wealth) to ensure that the value of the business grows over time. Unfortunately, many of us run our own personal finances like a poorly run company, where spending exceeds income and consumer (personal) debt accumulates. Consumer debt is things like owing on credit cards and car loans.

But here's the good news: we can use the strategies that well-run companies use to measure our own progress and frame our own financial situations. While we could delve into several different financial metrics, at this point, I want to narrow these metrics down to two fundamental financial statements. These are really all we need to measure and track our financial success:

-   **Income statement** – This shows the amount of money we are earning per pay period and the amount of money we are spending each pay period. If the difference is negative, then we're spending more than we're making and are likely running some form of consumer debt.
-   **Balance sheet** – This statement takes inventory of our assets (our car, our money sitting in the bank, any stocks we might have, etc.) and our liabilities (our debt). The net result is our net worth. We'll go into each of these in the following pages. If you don't have any assets right now, that's okay. I didn't at one point, either. But simply understanding what assets are is important, because eventually you *will* have assets.

These two financial statements are so critical to understand that we're going to spend some time really talking through them. Although none of this is hard to understand, it isn't typically taught in schools and largely isn't understood by a lot of people. That's why we're going to demystify these concepts and learn about them in the most basic of terms.

The personal finance section will also address the spending behavior we've been taught from birth and the way spending and keeping up with others have been ingrained into our lives. We live in a world of consumption, and we're taught to spend, whether on getting college degrees or cars or larger homes or all the things that fill up those homes. We have to break the cycle.

To be clear, I don't have any problem with spending money on the things we enjoy and value in life. If you have the financial means to drive a luxury car and park it in a large home in an exclusive part of town, then I'm genuinely happy for you.

Many of us who are reading this book will be in that club eventually, but many other people live this type of lifestyle on credit to give the illusion of wealth. They cannot actually afford to live that way—they always carry over their credit card balances and pay close to the minimum each month. Maybe you're currently in that situation yourself. That's the cycle we're going to break, but we have to first assess and understand our financial condition.

THE INCOME STATEMENT

In the most basic terms, the income statement is:

REVENUE
(INCOME FROM WORKING) **EXPENSES**
(MONEY WE SPEND ON THINGS) **NET INCOME**
(WHAT WE HAVE LEFT)

We must change our mindset and start to think of our personal financial situation as a business. The business is *us*, and we have revenue (i.e., income) coming into our business on a regular basis. Income can be generated from many sources, but in the most basic terms, it means **active income** that comes from doing work which we are then compensated for via an hourly rate or salary. Income can also be generated from **passive income**, which is income earned from an investment.

ACTIVE INCOME   **PASSIVE INCOME**

This type of income requires little actual effort or hours spent once the investment is owned and in place. We're going to talk a lot more about passive income in subsequent chapters, but for now, all we need to know is that it's simply an income stream from sources like rent collected from an investment property we own or a dividend from a stock we purchased. (You may not be anywhere close to thinking about stock returns, rental property income, or even owning a home. That's understandable. But it's important that you understand the concepts for the sake of your future self because you *will* have these options and that kind of lifestyle one day.)

Many of us will only have active income stemming from being employed by a company. Active income is how a great deal of us generate our revenue. The reason active income is so prevalent is because that's really all we're taught to seek as we grow up. "Achieve a certain level of schooling or learn a trade that employs and compensates you with a weekly paycheck," we hear. "Get up and do that each day." There's absolutely nothing wrong with generating active income as our only source of income—we can achieve our financial goals with this being our only source. But I want to open your mind to other sources of income, to other possibilities. Having multiple streams of income is the easiest way to truly achieve the pinnacle of financial success that's called "financial independence." We'll discuss financial independence later in the book.

Understanding Expenses

To recap, the first part of the income statement is revenue (Revenue - Expense = Net Income). This is the inflow of income (revenue) into our account via either active or passive income. Let us now talk about the next metric, which is our living expenses. Rent, mortgage, car payments, groceries, etc, are all examples of life expenses. We're much more immediate control of our expenses than we are of our income (revenue). This dynamic is why we simply must have a good understanding of where we spend our income.

Every business that is running on a sustainable basis monitors its expenses closely. If a well-run company finds that it's spending unnecessarily, it will immediately look to cut that expense. Business owners know they must do two things: find ways to grow income while reducing expenses. If a company generates $100 in income and pays bills and employees $99, then the owner of the company will have $1. For every dollar of expense that the company cuts, it will have one more dollar of net income. In personal finance terms, net income is simply the amount we're bringing in each month via active or passive income minus our expenses.

Well-run companies don't typically go out and buy the latest TV for the break room every year—that would reduce the amount of money the business is left with after expenses (i.e., its net income). So if well-run businesses don't waste money on the latest technology as soon as it comes out, then why do we, as consumers, do this? Because that's what other people have led us to believe is normal. It's also why most people never really meet their financial goals. Most people have financial dreams, not financial goals. Goals are achievable and require discipline to meet; dreams are speculative fantasies. Unfortunately, we could easily spend 20 years fantasizing and then wonder why we haven't attained financial success and the lifestyle we wish to live. Dreams are nonspecific and often unachievable.

It's critical to step back and start to think about the things we spend our money on. Are you one of the balance-carrying credit card customers who always purchase the latest phone or pair of shoes? People who carry over a monthly balance are called "revolvers." They have a revolving balance that carries over from month to month. If you're a revolver, you're not alone—about 55% of all credit cards have a balance that carries over from one month to the next.

Each month that our income is less than our expenses is another month when we have negative net income. Negative net income is where debt comes from, and it is a hard cycle to break unless we understand the game. The "game" is what society wants us to believe is normal. Commercials and influencers tell us what things we need to have in order to achieve the perception of success. Many consumers never fully understand that constantly purchasing such things robs them of being able to save early in the right investment vehicle, which in turn would allow them to live financially comfortably.

Even though we all have expenses, many of us don't really think about how we can manage them. Time to discuss the basic framework of how we can get a handle on our expenses! Expenses can generally be broken down into fixed costs and variable costs. Again, this is how a company views its expenses, and it's how we should run our own personal business in order to achieve financial success.

Let's start by talking about **fixed costs.** These don't go up or down as we live our lives. These are typically our housing costs (rent or mortgage payments), essential utilities (bills for electricity/water/internet/phone expenses), car expenses (insurance/car payments) and any other expense that we simply must pay to continue living. We cannot change our fixed costs at a moment's notice. If we want to reduce our fixed costs, we need to plan out alternatives in advance.

Fixed Costs

Rent / Mortgage / Car Payment

Variable Costs

Food / Clothes / Partying

Variable costs, on the other hand, go up and down based on our lifestyle. That means we can immediately reduce our variable costs by being mindful of our expenses and making different buying decisions. We're conditioned to go out and spend mindlessly on things we don't really need, often because we care about what others think of us, and we want to appear as though we're doing well. We have to break this mindset. It's not about having an expensive car. It's about maximizing our revenue and lowering our expenses to drive up our net income. But society doesn't talk about net income—we only see new cars and new jewelry and new clothes on Instagram. Society portrays having *things* as enviable.

Spending without purpose often happens because of the people we spend our time with or follow. Breaking the spending cycle might result in us spending less time with people who spend mindlessly. If we are surrounded by people who don't understand the concepts we're currently learning, then it will be difficult for us to change our spending habits. Cutting costs might make others around us feel uncomfortable, in part because we're making decisions that they themselves should probably be making but aren't.

If you're the most financially literate person in your circle or group, either positively influence the people around you or find a new group. You'll constantly be running up against resistance if you continue to be influenced by the consumerism mindset that many people have or show on social media. Many of the people closest to you might not be on board with your new mindset, so make sure you're setting yourself up for success by finding a group of people who will reinforce your new spending priorities. For example, that could be a group on Reddit whose members focus on personal finance and/or financial independence.

Some of your friends and family might conclude that your lack of spending means that you have lost your job or that you're maybe not as successful as they had thought. But I'm absolutely positive they will eventually seek your advice once you've achieved the financial success that lies in your future. It is just a matter of time!

We should acknowledge that our partner/spouse is an important person to have on board. Their views on spending will often times be a key factor in our ability to manage our expenses as a team. They might not be on board with this change in lifestyle, but we have to spend time syncing on this topic. Introduce your partner/spouse to this book! Get them excited about how these principles will change your life together forever! That might not happen immediately, but we must educate our significant others and set mutual goals. Our goals and their goals must be aligned. Going back to our discussion about how a well-run company is managed, we can't have managers (i.e., partners) who don't care about the business they're a part of.

Needs vs. Wants

These topics can be overwhelming at first, but they don't have to be. Like all things in life, we should only focus on the things that we can control. Fixed costs are out of our immediate control, so they should not be our initial focus. Instead, let's focus on daily variable costs. Go to your online banking platform and look at last month's expenses for your checking account and your credit card account(s). Make a list of fixed costs and variable costs, then spend some time thinking about the variable costs.

We're going to mindfully focus on the things that are needed by thinking of our variable spending in terms of "needs" and "wants." What are the things we need? Food, a car, clothing, etc. But we *want* to go out to dinner versus cook at home. We *want* the relatively new car that comes along with a higher car payment. We *want* the expensive brand-name clothing when we could go to Amazon for the basics.

We don't have to—and shouldn't—look for the cheapest item. We're better off purchasing based on value, meaning choosing the product that will last and can be purchased within our budget. A good example is the Honda Accord. It's not the cheapest car, but it's certainly not the most expensive, either. It's very practical and has lasting quality. I like what Benjamin Franklin said: "The bitterness of poor quality remains long after the sweetness of low price is forgotten."

Spending on "wants" comes from what others taught us. We were not born with a *want* for luxury clothing, but we were indeed born with the *need* for clothing. Other people teach us that we want the latest brands, styles, cars, homes, etc. Wants are often driven by us wanting to manage how others perceive us; needs are driven by what we actually need to live our lives.

Cutting expenses isn't easy, but we have to be willing to make sacrifices today to have freedoms and luxuries tomorrow. Being debt-free and able to live the lifestyle of our choosing is the eventual end game. That means we'll possibly need to stay in our small apartment or house for more years than we want to or even downsize from our current place. We might need to trade in our new expensive car with a big car payment for the 5- or 6-year-old Honda that we can buy with cash we've saved. Savings that result from delayed gratification multiply every year through compound interest. (More on that in a bit.) If we save early and regularly enough, eventually, we'll have enough income-producing assets to pay for our delayed wants in the future. We'll be able to use our assets to purchase our wants.

We should be incredibly careful when using today's dollars for today's wants. Wants should really only be satisfied once we've met our savings goals. One day, our income-producing assets—the ones we obtained and purchased through delayed gratification—will be used to pay for our daily wants. It's true that this scenario will likely be years and years away. But if we don't start thinking this way now, then being financially successful might never happen in our lifetime.

The ability to delay gratification is what separates the wealthy from the rest of the population. Delayed gratification is exactly what it sounds like: there *will* be a reward, but it will be delayed. The delay is the time when we accumulate wealth. The early stages of building our net worth happen the same way any other business starts: the first 10 years will be slow, but after that, net worth will quickly accelerate due to compounding interest. The initial focus is on building revenue (income) and keeping expenses low.

Don't waste today's resources on wants that are fleeting and that will rob Future You. Future You will benefit much more if you have that cash in an investment account as opposed to transforming it into a new pair of shoes. Future You will never be financially successful if you're not contributing to that person's success. Our future self is the only person we have complete control over; that person is the only person we can set up for a lifestyle that meets our current goals and expectations. The alternative is to live in the now and disregard the steps we need to take to enable that future person to exist. The choice is ours. And we need to be okay with our decision and own it because we're in complete control of who we become.

Hedonic Adaptation

While we're on the topic of "needs" and "wants," I'd like to introduce a concept that addresses the human nature of finding joy in materialist items...only to find that joy fades away once the prized possession is obtained. We've all experienced this—maybe we really wanted that new phone or that new pair of jeans, and once we have the item, we actually *do* feel a sense of reward and joy. That feeling might last a couple of hours or even a couple of days or weeks, but eventually, we're going to go back to feeling the same way we did before we purchased the item. The joy and the excitement wear off, and we go back to our "normal" level of happiness. This is true for both positive things in our life (like getting a new car) as well as for negative events (like losing a job).

This is referred to as "hedonic adaptation," and it's the reason why we always feel the need to have more and more. The joy from our latest new item is gone, and we think the next item will produce a more permanent level of joy. But the truth is that it won't. That next spark of joy will be just as fleeting as the last. It's true that we all have basic needs—food, shelter, clothing, security—but once those basic needs are met, then how much our joy level goes up or down is marginal and largely short-term.

A study published in the *Journal of Personality and Social Psychology* in 1978 titled "Lottery winners and accident victims: is happiness relative?" compared people who experienced great joy (lottery winners) and people who experienced great suffering (paraplegics from car accidents) to control groups. The researchers found that both the lottery winners and the car accident victims resettled to their stable levels of happiness. It's evidence that chasing the next new thing likely won't make a difference in our level of happiness. In fact, spending on that want will more often result in us regretting having purchased it after our short-term joy reverts back to baseline.

That said, this theory is nuanced. For example, if you have a car that's constantly breaking down and is a source of stress, then upgrading to a reliable vehicle can bring joy and can alleviate that stressor. The ensuing stress relief can bring ongoing satisfaction and appreciation. For the most part, though, once our basic needs are met, we've reached our stable level of happiness. We find short-term pleasure in things, yes, but we all gravitate back to our baseline. Purchasing an $85,000 BMW will not bring more sustainable joy than purchasing a used, reliable $15,000 Honda.

Hedonic adaptation also suggests that wealth doesn't increase our level of happiness. Having money doesn't make us happy—rather, money buys us options. Those options allow us to spend our time the way we want to spend it. Money gives us options like driving a reliable car and having shelter and security and peace of mind that we'll be able to handle adverse situations. It gives us options that ensure our needs will be met throughout our lives without us having to rely on others. But the luxury items that wealth affords don't equate to us having more joy in the long term.

Chasing the short-term joys of a materialistic world is how so many people get into financial indebtedness. Our brains are wired to believe that we need to get the next new thing because we think it will make us happy, and that mindset can put us on a treadmill that never ends—we're always striving for more and more, yet not attaining any meaningful, lasting joy or happiness. We constantly see proof of this with wealthy celebrities who live tragic, unhappy lives because their wealth didn't buy them happiness. That's because they became wealthy, and their baseline happiness was reset.

Lasting joy comes from liberty and the freedom to determine how we spend our time without the interference of other people or societal forces. There is an interesting lecture by Isaiah Berlin titled "Two Concepts of Liberty." The concepts of positive liberty and negative liberty are discussed. **Positive liberty** is when a person can be free of social inhibitions that interfere with carrying out their free will. The freedom from classism, racism, sexism, ageism, etc, are all examples of freedoms and liberties within the society we live and are considered positive liberty. **Negative liberty,** on the other hand, is the liberty to live one's life without interference from other people or outside factors. Being able to live your life without depending on trading your time for money is an example of negative liberty (like being financially independent). Negative liberty is also thought of as having the freedom and option to take advantage of opportunities. How many possible choices or options are available in one's life is also a measure of negative liberty. Maximizing both positive and negative liberties is believed to be the best way to achieve sustained happiness. Because with these two liberties, one can live the life one truly wants without any inhibitions. We'll talk about financial independence later in the guide, which will allow us to maximize our positive and negative liberties.

Putting these concepts aside, the fact is that the number one cause of stress for the majority of people is financial instability, and having a plan to live financially comfortably certainly helps to solve that. Now is our chance to put a plan in place to take this stressor off the table!

THE BALANCE SHEET

I've mentioned the term "assets" a few times, so let's talk about it more. Assets are a part of the second of two financial statements we absolutely need to understand. The first was the income statement. That looks at the amount of income we're bringing in minus our expenses, which results in our net income. If we spend more than we make, then we have a negative net income; if we spend less than what we earn, then we have a positive net income. The income statement is somewhat tactical, whereas the second financial statement—the balance sheet—is more strategic. The income statement allows us to assess our income and spending so that we can adjust our everyday spending. Having a command of our income and expenses will result in a positive net income. This positive net income is what drives balance sheet growth.

In the most basic terms, the balance sheet is:

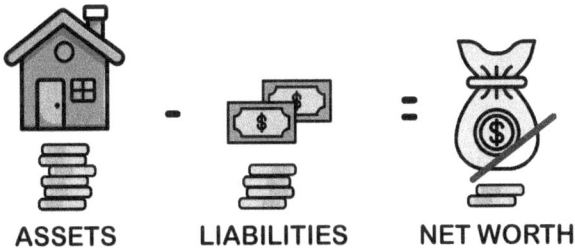

ASSETS   **LIABILITIES**   **NET WORTH**

Assets are the pieces of our financial statement that produce some form of income or have some form of value if sold. Assets can be stock we own once we start investing, for example. They can be rental properties we might own down the road or a cash-generating internet business we start. For this section, we're going to include our primary residence as an asset. Our car would also be an asset. Anything we own that has value to others—meaning another person would purchase the item—is an asset. Adding up all the items of value that we own constitutes our total assets.

You may not have many assets or any assets at all. That's okay! What we're talking about here is Future You. This might be the first time you've thought in these terms. Great! Now is a good time to get comfortable with these concepts.

Although many of us might not own any assets, I bet most of us have the other component of the balance sheet: liabilities. **Liabilities** are simply the debts we owe someone else, like our credit card balance or the amount left on our car or student loan. Liabilities are anything we will eventually have to pay back. People who have a mortgage would include the loan amount as a liability on their personal balance sheet. For a company, liabilities are also the expenses (debt) they pay, like a bank loan or the payroll the business must pay at the end of each month.

Balance sheet statements are always a point in time, and our balance sheet constantly changes because our assets are always going up or down—we're either paying off or accumulating liabilities. The key figure on the balance sheet is the result of our assets minus our liabilities: namely, our net worth. Net worth is the standard for measuring financial wealth, whether that be large or small or positive or negative. It's all the things we own minus all the money we owe someone else.

Let's say we eventually are homeowners. If our home is valued at $100,000 but we still owe the bank $75,000, our net worth would be $25,000, assuming we had no other assets or liabilities.

Net Income vs. Net Worth

Being wealthy isn't about how much money we make—it's about how much net worth we have. People with high-earning jobs might be "rich" because they can live a luxurious lifestyle, but they aren't necessarily "wealthy" because if they don't have any income-producing assets, they can't survive without that elusive high-paying job. Someone who makes $250,000 per year in income and has $240,000 in expenses has a net income (not a net worth) of $10,000. If they lost that $250,000 job, then they'd still very likely need to find the $240,000 per year that affords them the lifestyle they've become accustomed to.

It's important to regularly measure our net income and ensure that we're not spending more than we make. The eventual goal is to use our positive net income to accumulate assets or pay down debt, all of which will increase our net worth. Our net worth is a measure of how long we can live without having to work. Put differently, if our net worth is high enough, then our income-producing assets will produce an annual income stream that can meet the costs related to our chosen lifestyle. Keep in mind that we also need to have low liabilities because the goal is to have a high net income. We want to have income produced by passive income streams so that we can eventually live without worrying about active income (i.e., a 9-to-5 job). This is years down the road, but we need to start considering these outcomes as possibilities for us.

Recall that there are two forms of income: **active income** (work you get paid for, like your job) and **passive income** (income that comes from your investments). The ultimate goal is for our passive income to produce enough income to pay for our expenses. This concept isn't taught in formal schooling, so most people don't really understand the necessary framework they need to have to accomplish this. Those who reach this financial status don't have to get up and work a job they don't like—they have the financial strength to choose how they spend their time. This is what we call financial independence.

Maybe being financially independent isn't your goal. That works, too...but everyone needs to have a plan for retirement at some point, and understanding these principles can help you achieve an eventual comfortable retirement. At a minimum, you need to be ready for the inevitable reality that you won't be able to (or want to) work at some point in your life.

LIFE PRO TIP *To me, delayed gratification is about deciding when you want to struggle with money. Do you want to save and have a very tight budget early in life so that you're set up for the future? Or do you want to struggle later in life because you didn't go through the struggle earlier by saving? Either way, you're going to have to adjust your spending. The tip here is that if you choose to struggle earlier in life (by saving a lot of your income), then the rewards are much more meaningful later in life compared to spending now and struggling later. If you do the hard things now, then your life will become easier...but if you do the easy things now, then your life will likely get harder.*

CREATING A PERSONAL BUDGET

Now that we've discussed how to create our personal income statements and balance sheets, let's discuss the basics of developing a budget. First, we need to identify our fixed household expenses and our variable household expenses; then, we'll further break down our variable household expenses into "needs" and "wants." Again, needs are our basic needs, like shelter, food, clothing, etc. Wants are the things we desire but don't really require. Notice that there are a number of expenses we might not have today, but if we let our lifestyle "creep" as our income increases, then we'll inevitably have more and more expenses eating into our net income.

Lifestyle creep is a trap many of us fall into—we consume more and more as our income grows. Society encourages us to just go ahead and spend money on things we think are important, and the more money we make, the more we tend to do this. We need to get on a track that will allow us to grow professionally and increase our income while at the same time increasing our savings rate. This is delayed gratification at its finest! Sure, you could spend that extra couple hundred dollars per month you got from a promotion on a new car payment. *Or* you could ignore the increase in pay and put the extra into your savings. Maybe you won't be living the exact lifestyle you want to have if you increase your savings and don't spend more, but that's temporary. Your gratification is just delayed—you'll eventually enjoy the benefits once your income-producing assets support your desired lifestyle. Developing a budget and committing to increasing your savings rate over time is the path to financial success and financial independence.

Balancing a budget is the very first step toward financial success, so let's start with the basics. In order to develop your budget, you'll need to take inventory of all of your expenses and break them down into fixed costs, variable costs that are needed (needs), and variable costs that are wanted (wants). The example below outlines the typical line items that go into a budget. This initial assessment of our expenses might be surprising to many of us—most people don't really know where their money goes throughout the month, and very few lay out their budget and work to lower their costs in order to maximize their savings.

While it's more enjoyable *not* to have to worry about the budget, *not* worrying about where our money goes will eventually translate into worrying about the fact that we have nothing saved 20 years down the line. We can live our lives without any planning, but one day we will look back and wish we had managed things differently...and it will be too late at that point. We will have lost years of possible compounding interest from investments, and we'll be in a much more stressful position because our options will be limited at that point. If we take the time to tackle our expenses now and develop a budget now, we will be enabling our future selves to be financially secure. But if our current selves don't set up our future selves, we'll never really become financially comfortable, let alone financially independent.

Once we've developed our budget, it's important to regularly update it with actual results and adjust it over time. "Plan the work and then work the plan" should be our motto. An effective approach for many people is to set aside funds for various buckets of expenses. If we have $400 per month budgeted for groceries, for example, we'll keep those funds in a wallet marked "Groceries" and use it throughout the month for groceries.

Many people find using credit cards to be too easy, and they consequently run up a balance they can't pay off each month. The negative number simply accrues (grows) via a credit card balance that gets bigger every month because people spend more than they make. It's a very dangerous trap to fall into. It's also an *easy* trap to fall into because credit card companies make it very easy to do so with their minimum payment strategy. (More on that later.) A large portion of households spends more than they make and keep doing so for years. All the while, the household is living their best life, but it's a lifestyle that's beyond their financial means. Eventually, it catches up to them. By then, they have tens of thousands of dollars in credit card debt and few ways of paying it off. Even worse, as the credit card balance grows, even more income is needed to pay the minimum payment on the credit card, meaning that the household has less cash to spend on their needs...which means the credit card is used even more. This is a cycle we want to avoid at all costs.

A thoughtful budget also highlights where our money is going. If we have a car payment that accounts for a substantial amount of our monthly spending and we then don't have enough cash to dedicate to savings, we should strongly consider making some tough decisions about whether the car is worth the monthly financial commitment. (There's also car insurance to consider.) Is it worth working until the day we die in order to drive an expensive, depreciating asset when an older model would be a very viable option? Are we okay with making the sacrifice today to have security later? And we shouldn't worry about what other people think. People who matter and care about us would much rather see us realize financial security than have an expensive car or brand-name jeans. People who are really rooting for us would encourage us to save and would support us as we make better financial decisions. Put differently, when it comes to spending on a big luxurious lifestyle, the people that care about our lifestyle don't typically matter, and the people that matter don't typically care.

Nobody will ever say that purchasing expensive items we can't afford is a good idea, but people *will* quietly watch us overspend because they're likely also overspending and embracing the YOLO mentality. However, anybody who has found financial success will tell you that living above your means leads to problems down the road. We need to do the same and set our future selves up for more than what our current selves have. A number of online tools can help us develop a budget—there are endless resources, including free online platforms and apps for our mobile devices.

LIFE PRO TIP *An "easy" way to manage lifestyle creep is to set up automated withdrawals from your checking account into your savings account. Automatically saving removes the effort so that you're not tempted to spend more. Make the automatic deduction from your checking account happen the same day you get paid so the funds are always saved. Increase the automatic savings rate as your pay increases over time.*

HOUSEHOLD BUDGET TEMPLATE	MONTHLY BUDGET	MONTHLY ACTUAL	DIFFERENCE
HOUSEHOLD INCOME (MONTHLY)			
TAKE-HOME SALARY FROM EMPLOYER (AFTER ALL DEDUCTIONS)*	$ 4,000.00	$ 4,000.00	$ -
PASSIVE INCOME (RENTAL PROPERTIES / DIVIDENDS / ETC.)	$ -	$ -	$ -
TOTAL INCOME	$ 4,000.00	$ 4,000.00	$ -
HOUSEHOLD EXPENSES (MONTHLY)			
FIXED NEEDS (BASIC EXPENSES OUT OF YOUR SHORT-TERM CONTROL)			
HOUSING (RENT OR MORTGAGE PAYMENT)	$ 1,100.00	$ 1,100.00	$ -
ELECTRICITY	$ 75.00	$ 75.00	$ -
WATER	$ 20.00	$ 20.00	$ -
PHONE	$ 50.00	$ 50.00	$ -
INTERNET SERVICE	$ 50.00	$ 50.00	$ -
MAINTENANCE	$ 50.00	$ 50.00	$ -
CAR INSURANCE	$ 50.00	$ 50.00	$ -
VARIABLE NEEDS (BASIC EXPENSES IN YOUR CONTROL)			
GROCERIES	$ 400.00	$ 395.00	$ 5.00
PERSONAL SUPPLIES	$ 40.00	$ 30.00	$ 10.00
BASIC CLOTHING	$ 40.00	$ 100.00	$ (60.00)
PERSONAL CARE (HAIR / COSMETICS / ETC.)	$ 40.00	$ 50.00	$ (10.00)
CAR: GAS / MAINTENANCE	$ 100.00	$ 95.00	$ 5.00
OTHER	$ 50.00	$ 20.00	$ 30.00

WANTS (VARIABLE EXPENSE BY DEFINITION)			
VACATION (BUILDING UP THE GETAWAY FUND)	$ 50.00	$ 50.00	-
EATING OUT / GOING OUT	$ 25.00	$ 25.00	-
BRAND-NAME CLOTHING	$ 25.00	$ -	25.00
ENTERTAINMENT (ACTIVITIES / GAMES / HOBBIES / ETC.)	$ 100.00	$ 75.00	25.00
CHILDREN			
CLOTHING	$ -	$ -	-
DAY CARE	$ -	$ -	-
SCHOOL LUNCH	$ -	$ -	-
BABYSITTING	$ -	$ -	-
EXTRA-CURRICULAR - SPORTS / MUSICAL INSTRUMENTS / ETC.)	$ -	$ -	-
SAVINGS			
EMERGENCY FUND (CONTRIBUTE UNTIL YOU MEET 3 MNTH. EXP.)	$ 50.00	$ 100.00	(50.00)
SAVINGS (IRA / PURCHASING STOCKS / PURCHASING REAL ESTATE)	$ -	$ -	-
EDUCATION FUND (NOT AT THE EXPENSE OF RETIREMENT SAVINGS)	$ -	$ -	-
DEBT OBLIGATIONS			
STUDENT LOANS	$ 400.00	$ 400.00	-
CREDIT CARD REPAYMENT (STARTING WITH HIGHEST INTEREST)	$ 500.00	$ 350.00	150.00
CAR PAYMENT (IDEALLY YOU TRADE IN THE PAYMENT FOR A USED VEHICLE)	$ 500.00	$ 450.00	50.00
TOTAL EXPENSES	$ 3,715.00	$ 3,535.00	180.00
NET (INCOME - EXPENSES)	$ 285.00	$ 465.00	180.00

* DEDUCTIONS INCLUDE FEDERAL TAXES / STATE & LOCAL TAXES / SOCIAL SECURITY / MEDICARE / HEALTH INSURANCE / 401K CONTRIBUTIONS

A 7-STEP PLAN – YOUR GUIDE TO WHERE YOUR SAVINGS SHOULD GO

Many people want a clear plan around where they should start their financial journey and how they should handle their cash differently. We're going to talk through 7 clear steps that can be followed sequentially. The steps are pretty straightforward, yet not commonly understood. Within the steps, you'll see that there are a variety of investment buckets that act as a "waterfall," where the first savings bucket (your emergency fund) needs to get filled first; then, once that's filled, you fill the second bucket (matched 401k); then, once that's filled, we move to the third bucket, and so on. Below are the 7 steps as well as a list of investment vehicles or investment "buckets" that you'll fill. We'll discuss each of these in detail, but here's the list:

1. **Optimize your active income** through your employer and find a side hustle or part-time job while reducing your fixed and variable costs.
2. Open a separate checking or savings account with your bank and **start an emergency fund** equaling 3 months of expenses.
3. **Contribute to your employer's 401k** at least up to the employer match.
4. **Pay down consumer debt** and especially target the debt carrying the highest interest rates.
5. **Open and fund a Roth IRA account** with Fidelity or a brokerage firm of your choice (IRA = individual retirement account).
6. **Invest in other assets** like maxing 401k contributions over employer match, investing in rental properties or nonretirement brokerage accounts that invest in low-fee index funds like FSKAX (total market mutual fund).
7. **Fund your children's Education** *OPTIONAL BUCKET:* If paying for your child's (or future

child) higher education is a primary goal, then you can now use proceeds to fund their 529 plan.

a. Keep in mind that while there are plenty of loan programs for students to use to borrow educational funds, absolutely no bank will give you a loan for retirement. Fund your retirement first, then consider helping with your child's college expenses.

b. The seventh bucket is also where you can contribute to a Health Savings Account, but this is only applicable to those whose employers offer it. A Health Savings Account is different than a Healthcare Spending Account in that with a Healthcare *Spending* Account, you have to use all of the money you contribute to it each calendar year. With a Health *Savings* Account, on the other hand, you can accumulate funds over time and you can use it during retirement with tax-free dollars.

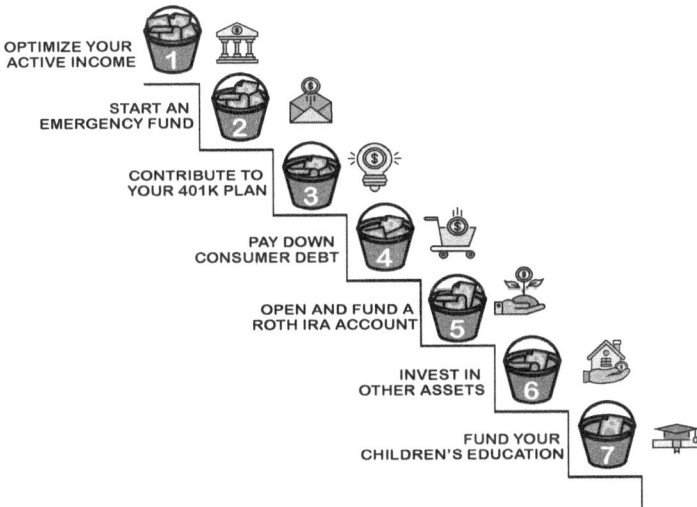

OPTIMIZE YOUR ACTIVE INCOME **1**

START AN EMERGENCY FUND **2**

CONTRIBUTE TO YOUR 401K PLAN **3**

PAY DOWN CONSUMER DEBT **4**

OPEN AND FUND A ROTH IRA ACCOUNT **5**

INVEST IN OTHER ASSETS **6**

FUND YOUR CHILDREN'S EDUCATION **7**

I know that's an exhaustive list and that maybe some of those items seem far-fetched. 401k? Who has that? Actually, over 65% of the population winds up participating in an employer 401k program at some point, so chances are you will eventually have the opportunity to participate in one yourself. It's good to learn about this now so that you'll know what you can do when a 401k *is* available to you. It's important to stay optimistic about the future and expect to have plenty of opportunities!

Step #1 – Optimizing Your Household Income Statement

The journey to financial success starts with managing our income statement, meaning thinking through ways we can maximize our income while reducing our fixed costs and taking an axe to our variable wants. Managing our expenses, particularly at the beginning of our financial journey, is important for two reasons: it allows us to save for investment purposes, and it also helps us establish a lifestyle that is within our means. Starting off, we're likely not going to have a very high salary unless we're maybe in technology or finance. Still, regardless of our job or salary, it's important to develop a budget that allows us to have money left over each month to dedicate to developing our balance sheet and growing our assets.

We'll use a budget to help develop our income statement. In fact, the actual income statement is pretty much the same thing as a budget. They both look at what's coming in (cash earned through active or passive income) and then look at the expenses that chew up that income. Our budget (or income statement) is a living document, meaning that we need to continually track our progress and update our budget accordingly.

While we've already talked about what makes up the income statement and how to think about developing our budget, we haven't spent much time talking about the income side of the income statement. When we're just starting out in life, we likely have more free time than those who might have already established a family with kids and other responsibilities. It's during these initial stages of our lives—as we graduate from formal schooling—that we can work side hustles that produce income over and above our 9-to-5 job. A side hustle is anything that provides an alternate income stream in addition to a career job, like a part-time job at a hotel or driving an Uber. Or a side hustle could be making things at home and selling them on Etsy.

I had a part-time job until the age of around 26. I would get off my full-time job and then work a 6-to-9 p.m. shift at a call center. I knew I would still have free time after work and on the weekends, so I felt it was a perfect way to supplement my income while keeping me busy so that I didn't have a *ton* of free time to spend more money—then I would actually be earning and not spending. (I found that when left to my own devices, I would often just spend more money.) I knew that working part-time would be a surefire way of not only *not* spending but also adding to my savings.

It's smart to plan a way to maximize our income during our early savings years when we can use the energy of youth to maximize our savings early on and then enjoy the maximum benefits of compounding interest. Time is a critical component of compounding interest! It's never too early to think about that and act to take advantage of time. The fact that you're even reading this book and strategically planning your future puts you miles ahead of your peers, so you're on the right track.

LIFE PRO TIP *It's easier to make an extra $10,000 per year than it is to cut expenses by $10,000 – the sooner this is understood and put into practice, the sooner we'll reach our financial goals.*

Step #2 – Establishing an Emergency Fund

You may have read that around 54% of Americans live paycheck to paycheck and that many could not cover a $500 out-of-the-blue expense. That's why establishing an emergency fund is important—we don't know what the future holds. Back in January 2020, no one had any idea of what was about to hit just one month later when COVID-19 spread around the world. Many people quickly lost what they thought were very stable jobs.

In establishing my own emergency fund, I've found it helpful to have a separate checking account dedicated to holding 3 months' worth of expenses. Some people suggest up to 6 months of savings—and that certainly can't hurt—but I recommend you start with 3 months. Once you have it saved, just don't touch it.

Step #1 should provide you with some breathing room and increased net income because you will have lowered your expenses and found additional income through your side hustle. Use this additional net income to build an emergency fund safety net. Knowing that you wouldn't be out on the streets should something drastic happen to your active income source will provide you with peace of mind. The emergency fund will also ensure that you're not reliant on others to step in when you have unexpected financial obligations.

Step #3 – Investing in a 401k

The average person will start their asset accumulation phase the same way I did, through active income stemming from an employer. An employer will generally offer two types of retirement benefit plans:

- **Defined Contribution Plan** – This is a plan that has tax benefits because you fund the plan yourself. This is your 401k plan.
- **Defined Benefit Plan** – This plan is funded by

your employer in the form of a pension. These plans are very rare nowadays and have not generally been offered since the invention of the 401k. You will, though, find pension plans still in place with many State or Federal employers.

The typical employer (upwards of 65% of US employers) offers a defined contribution plan in the form of a 401k. Funding our 401k up to the employer match is where we should start. The employer's HR resource can help you set up a 401k plan. You'll want to invest the cash you put into the 401k plan in diversified index funds. But you can't just pick any fund—your employer chooses what's called a plan administrator (think Fidelity or ADP or Charles Schwab), and that administrator offers a set of funds that you can invest in. Find a fund that has a large, diverse set of companies. Most employers offer something like an S&P500 index. Much like it sounds, this kind of index invests in the largest 500 companies in the US. This is what is called a "domestic fund" because it only contains US companies. You'll likely also see an "international fund," which invests in nondomestic companies outside of the US (think Siemens or BMW or Sony). It's always a good idea to have international diversification, so I typically choose 85% domestic (like an S&P500 fund) and then 15% international.

Let's talk about the "company match" concept. Most employers offer a match anywhere between 2% to 6%. When you set up your 401k, you'll be asked what percentage contribution you want to allocate to be deducted from your paycheck. If your employer offers, say, a 3% match, then at a minimum, you want to set up your 401k deduction to that same percentage. What this means is that if you make $50,000 per year and you use a 3% contribution rate, then you will have 3% taken out of your paycheck before taxes, and that amount will be deposited into your 401k account. In my example, that would be $1,500 per year, so if you're paid every other week, that would be around

$28.85 per paycheck ($28.85 x 52 weeks = $1,500).

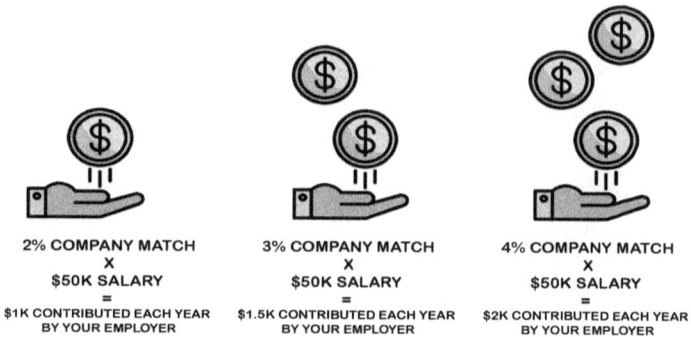

2% COMPANY MATCH	3% COMPANY MATCH	4% COMPANY MATCH
X	X	X
$50K SALARY	$50K SALARY	$50K SALARY
=	=	=
$1K CONTRIBUTED EACH YEAR BY YOUR EMPLOYER	$1.5K CONTRIBUTED EACH YEAR BY YOUR EMPLOYER	$2K CONTRIBUTED EACH YEAR BY YOUR EMPLOYER

Because your employer matches up to 3% in my example, then your employer will also deposit the same $1,500 into your 401k account. This is free money. You can contribute more to your 401k—say, 4%—but your employer will only match up to 3%. They won't match the extra 1% that you're contributing over their match. Again, employers have different benefit plans—some offer a 2% match, some offer up to a 6% match, and some don't offer a match at all. You want to contribute at least to your employer match so that you're fully leveraging their willingness to contribute to your retirement.

I'll add that many employers have rules around the length of time employees have to work at the company in order to enjoy the employer match. Some companies, for instance, require that you are an employee for a year before they'll start matching. You can likely still make contributions to your 401k during your first year, but it won't start getting matched until after your first 12 months. Again, this is something you can ask your company's HR resource about.

Let's uptick the concepts and get into a more AP-level discussion. I mentioned that, typically, your 401k contributions are deducted from your paycheck before taxes. For the sake of discussion, we'll say you earn $50,000 per year and contribute 3% to your 401k. If you get paid every 2 weeks, then that's

$961.53 gross every 2 weeks ($50k / 52 weeks = $961.53).

As discussed above, $28.85 will be deducted from each paycheck if you contribute 3% to your 401k. That $28.85 will be reduced from the before-tax amount of $961.53. This is important because this means that if you pay, say, 20% as your federal tax rate, then your tax burden is reduced by $1,500 per year. Because it's "before taxes," the amount you're taxed on is reduced by your 401k contribution.

In my example of a 20% federal tax rate on an income of $50,000, you'd pay $10,000 in federal taxes ($50,000 x 20% = $10,000). But because you contributed $1,500 to your 401k, your taxable income goes from $50,000 down to $48,500. That means you pay 20% of $48,500, which equals $9,700 and not the $10,000 that you would pay if you didn't contribute to your 401k.

	NO 401K CONTRIBUTION	3% 401K CONTRIBUTION
TAXABLE INCOME	$50,000	$50,000
401K CONTRIBUTION	-	$1,500
NEW TAXABLE INCOME	$50,000	$48,500
INCOME TAXES PAID (20% RATE)	$10,000	$9,700

You have therefore reduced the amount you pay the federal government by $300 per year because you contributed to your 401k. That adds up! If you're not contributing up to your employer match, then you're missing out on an additional $1,500 from them (3% of your $50,000 salary) *plus* your reduced tax bill of $300. That equals $1,800 per year that you're missing out on!

You can see why it's so important to start making contributions to your 401k right away, going at least up to the employer match. It's also worth pointing out that the employer match part (the

3% in our example) does not impact your personal taxable income either in a positive or a negative way. From a tax perspective, it's as if the employer match didn't occur. (The match *does* have a positive tax benefit for your employer, though—they can reduce their net income by the amount they've contributed to their employees' 401k plans.) So the tax burden on the $1,500 employer match in our example does not impact your personal taxes. You *don't* pay taxes on the employer's $1,500 match in our 3% match example.

Your 401k also has the benefit of growing each year tax-free, meaning that as long as you keep the funds in a 401k, they grow without you paying taxes over the years. You can sell and purchase mutual funds within the 401k plan and only pay taxes when the funds are withdrawn at retirement. You can draw from your 401k at around age 60, although that age is subject to change. You can search the latest rules around this by looking up "401k age withdrawal."

I know life happens, but avoid withdrawing from your 401k at all costs! If you do, you'll pay a 10% tax penalty over and above the standard tax rate. Don't withdraw funds from your 401k unless it's absolutely critical. Once you start to make 401k withdrawals, provided you've met the minimum age requirement for withdrawals, the withdrawals are taxed at a normal taxable income, as though you were earning the money from your employer.

Your 401k will likely be your largest pool of retirement savings, so it's critical to start contributing to it as soon as you have the chance to do so.

Step #4 – Paying Down Consumer Debt

This is where it starts to get fun! Paying down debt is an amazing feeling once we're on the path. That said, it's very hard at the beginning, largely because most people don't really want to know what their total debt is—it's much easier to only pay the minimum amount and not think about the bigger picture. But it's critical to get our hands around our debt (our liabilities) in order to make any progress. Yes, it might be scary at first, and these are topics a lot of people don't want to address—that's why most just let the balance on their credit cards roll over from one month to the next. It might seem too large to worry about, prompting us to continue to delay any action; maybe when we do start to think about our debt, anxiety hits. If you don't have any consumer debt because you haven't racked up a meaningful balance or you've just never used debt, keep it that way. You'll be much better off if you avoid doing that!

But the reality is that most of us have consumer debt in the form of credit cards, car loans, payday loans, or some other form of consumer borrowing. (Avoid payday loans at all costs!! Those carry interest rates in the 29.9%+ range!!) Notice I did not include a primary household mortgage in with what we're referring to as consumer debt. That's because buying a home is a form of "good debt" as long as we can comfortably afford the monthly mortgage payment. We'll go into more detail regarding buying a home later in the book.

It's important to understand why consumer debt is a trap we want to avoid. The real problem with consumer debt is the high interest rates we pay for borrowing the money. When we establish a consumer loan, we have the principal amount that we've borrowed, which is also the amount that we ultimately have to pay back. As we finance the loan—meaning we don't actually pay it back immediately but rather hold a balance—we will be assessed interest on our principal. This Principal & Interest (P&I) concept is important to understand because it holds true for basically all forms of consumer debt.

Credit Cards

Credit card companies often encourage consumers to pay as little as possible on their credit card balances via the concept of a "minimum payment." Often, the credit card company will calculate the minimum payment to be the interest component plus generally 1% to 2% of the principal. If you have a credit card balance of $10,000 and your interest rate is 15.99%, then your monthly minimum payment might be:

$100	**$136**	**$236**
TOWARDS PRINCIPAL	IN INTEREST	MONTHLY PAYMENT
$10,000 BALANCE x 1% IN PRINCIPAL PAYBACK	(15.99% INTEREST RATE/ 365 DAYS PER YEAR) x 31 DAYS IN THE MONTH	

Take note of how the interest is typically calculated: it's the interest rate divided by the number of days in the year, then multiplied by the number of days in the payment month. This is typically how interest is calculated across all consumer debt. Consumer debt refers to the interest rate as the APR (Annual Percentage Rate), but that annual rate is broken down to a daily rate by dividing by 365, then multiplied by the number of days in the given (current) month that the payment is due. The other point is that if our balance is low enough, then our minimum payment is typically a minimum of $25. In the above formula, the $10,000 x 1% is the amount we're paying toward the principal, which is $100. The rest of the $236 payment is going to the interest costs of carrying a balance. That means that *over half of your monthly payment is interest.* We can see just how costly it is to live over our means and run consumer debt. It's very expensive to carry consumer debt! And that debt is, in many instances, related to "wants" spending.

Paying only the minimum payment is a trap we can get stuck in for quite literally decades. **It can take 15 or 20 years to pay off a balance if we only pay the minimum pay-**

ment. Why? Because we're only paying off 1% of the principal each month, and it takes a long time to chip away at the principal if we're only paying 1 or 2% each time. But consumer debt payments typically allow us to pay more than the minimum payment, and any additional payment over the minimum payment goes directly against the principal. **We can really chip away at the principal by paying more than the minimum payment.**

One word of advice regarding paying more than the minimum payment: some companies are getting cute with making a payment that's greater than the minimum due. In these cases, the overpayment goes toward next month's payment and does not actually reduce the principal. For example, if your minimum payment is $100 and you pay $125, then the extra $25 is credited to next month's minimum payment, making it $75. The extra $25 did not reduce the principal as you had intended it to. By lowering next month's minimum payment, the bank keeps your principal the same and simply reduces the next minimum payment by the extra $25. That means you're prepaying next month's interest rather than making a principal-only contribution. We want the extra payment to drive down the principal, not make an early payment toward next month's payment! It's important to understand these dynamics, which you can research by calling your bank. I do not personally like to do business with banks that play games like this.

Let's talk about some of the other tactics that credit card companies use to keep consumers on the debt treadmill. One popular offering is the balance transfer, which often has a 0% interest rate for maybe up to 12 months. A balance transfer is where we open up a credit card with one company with the intention of moving (transferring) a balance from another credit card to the new one to reduce our interest payment. This can be a powerful tool, but only if we pay off the credit card debt on the new balance transfer before the promotional window expires. If we don't totally pay off the balance transfer within the promotional window, then—still using my example of 12 months— typically the interest starting from 12 months ago is added to our principal. That's right! The fine print often states that the 0% is only appliable if there's a zero balance once the promotional window has concluded.

Another tactic banks use is the cash advance option. Cash advances are almost always charged a 19.99% interest rate or more—in other words, way more than a standard purchase rate. Let's step back for a moment. There are typically two interest rates for two different types of balances on most credit cards: one rate and balance for standard purchases at stores and a second (higher!) rate for balances related to cash advances. Cash advances are where we use our credit cards to take cash out of an ATM. Banks consider these transactions to be riskier because it's a clear indicator that the cardholder is struggling with cash flow and might not be able to pay back what they borrowed. The tricky part is that while many banks will allow us to make the cash advance, our future payments go toward our purchase balance and not the cash advance balance. So if we have a balance of $1,000 and we take a cash advance for $100, then our next payment will help lower the $1,000 principal balance, which has a lower standard purchase interest rate. The $100 balance for the cash advance sits there at the higher rate until the balance of the $1,000 is paid off. Only then does our payment go to the $100 cash advance. That means we can carry the cash advance balance with a 19.99% interest rate for years! But here's the good news: **we can avoid all of this by not taking cash advances. Ever.**

Credit cards can be a great tool *if* we have the discipline to pay off the balance each month. When we use the card and pay off the balance each month, we're simply a transactor. The cardholder typically doesn't pay any interest or fees if the balance related to store purchases is paid in full. But remember that this is not the case for cash advances—cash advances accrue interest starting the day we take the cash from the ATM. Even if it's a best-case scenario and we pay off the cash advance balance at the end of the month, we are still charged for the interest at a rate of 19.99% (or more) for the days that we had an outstanding cash advance balance.

LIFE PRO TIP *If you have a large credit card balance that includes a cash advance component, look to get a balance transfer with another credit card provider so you can pay off the balance of the card that has the purchase balance and the cash advance balance. This way, the entire balance moves to a new card and is considered a balance transfer, and you'll avoid the high cash advance rate on the card balance you're transferring. Just remember to work hard to pay down the balance transfer before the intro rate has expired in order to avoid being charged all of the interest. The intro rate is typically good for 6, 12, or 24 months, depending on the offer.*

You might have heard about "charge cards." The difference between a charge card and a credit card is that the charge card isn't designed to carry a balance. There's no credit limit for a charge card. If we don't pay it off each month, then we'll be charged an enormous interest rate as well as a substantial late fee. Credit cards are designed to have a credit component and are there to encourage running a balance. American Express is one of the few companies still offering a charge card.

So what happens if we run up a credit card bill and then stop making payments? First off, the credit card company will charge us a late fee and happily accrue (add to) the interest we didn't pay. If we're delinquent past about 60 days, then we'll start to get calls from the bank's Collections Department. If the bank's Collections Department isn't able to get us back on track with paying back the balance, then after 3 to 4 months of attempts, our debt will be considered "nonperforming" and likely sold to a collections agency that purchases consumer debt for pennies on the dollar. That means that if we owe $100 and the collections agency purchases our nonperforming debt, they might only pay $25 or $30 for our $100 balance. The original bank that gave us the credit card then writes off the difference between our balance and what the collections agency purchased it for.

Banks set funds aside and refer to these funds as "loan loss provisions," which is just another way of saying that these funds are earmarked for customers who don't pay back their loan or debt. Banks continue to add to their loan loss provisions through the interest they charge their customers. The reason that 19.99% interest rate is so high is because the bank has to set aside part of the interest we pay them to cover losses from other customers who default on their debt. This is why consumers who have poor credit have higher interest rates—the chance of a customer with poor credit not paying off their credit card is higher than someone who has a history of never having been late on making their payments.

Now, I'm not suggesting that charging interest rates in the 19.99% to 29.99% range isn't taking advantage of people struggling with credit. There will, though, always be a higher rate for consumers with poor credit simply because their risk of not paying back the lender is higher. We'll talk about credit scores in another chapter, but I'll say now is that our credit score is very important and sticks with us for life. Loans we default on stay on our credit report for up to approximately 7 years before they drop off. Paying a bill late is reported to credit agencies right away, so it's really important to keep a "clean" credit score. More on this topic later.

If we have defaulted on a loan and the balance is already with a collections agency (meaning the bank already sold it for pennies on the dollar), then we can work with the agency and often times agree on a reduced balance (amount owned). That's because they might have paid $25 for that $100 balance we defaulted on, and anything they collect over $25 is profit to them. We won't know how much the agency paid, but we can be sure that it was some reduced amount, so negotiating is important. If we defaulted on a loan more than 7 years ago, then a collections agency might still call because the debt is often sold to yet another collections agency after the first one. The second collections agency might have paid only $10 for that same debt. The older the debt, the less chance it will be collected, so it becomes less and less valuable as the debt is sold off.

Eventually, a collections agency might pay only a couple of dollars for that debt, so they'll try calling us well after 7 years past the original default. Just know that after 7 years, the debt falls off our credit report, so although a collections agency might threaten and continue to call, they really can't do anything to our credit score (if it's after 7 years). Be careful when engaging with an agency if you're close to or have passed the seven-year mark for a specific defaulted loan—there are instances where a consumer makes a deal with an agency after the 7 years have passed and their actions actually reset the 7 years.

Be careful when dealing with these agencies, and get everything in writing! Don't just believe what you're told by the collections agency. They do not have your best interests in mind. It's also a good idea to conduct all communications with the agency in writing. You can request a "debt validation letter" from the agency in writing, which they, in turn, will mail back. If you do end up negotiating a settlement amount, make sure you get a written statement that the debt has been paid in full. Some agencies will accept your settlement payment and only deduct that amount from your balance and then possibly sell the remaining balance to another agency. So make sure you get everything in writing, including written confirmation that the debt has been settled. Seek professional credit advice if you find yourself in a collections situation that you can't sort out on your own. The key here is to understand the debt you have out to collections agencies and understand when the defaulted loan will eventually be removed from your score. If your credit report incorrectly shows a defaulted loan, you will need to work with the specific agency to get it rectified.

More on credit scores and credit agencies later, but for now, just understand that defaulted consumer debt sticks on our credit report for 7 years, and we'll likely be harassed by collections agencies during that time.

Auto Loans

Auto loans are another form of consumer debt that has its own nuances and pitfalls. The first one is the terms of the loan, so that's where we'll start. Specifically, let's talk about the tenor (or time frame) of the loan. In the 1990s, the typical auto loan was between 36 to 48 months (3 to 4 years). Car loans are now typically 72 to 84 months, so many people will be making their car payments for 6 to 7 years. Because cars have become increasingly more reliable, banks feel more comfortable with lending at that tenor because the repossession value is higher now than it was in the 90s. These days, if we default in Year 6 of our 84-month loan, when the bank repossesses (takes away) the car and sells it at auction, chances are they won't take a big loss because the vehicle will still hold value.

Another key reason the tenor is so long is that most consumers are only worried about their monthly payment amount. The monthly payment amount can be quite low if it's stretched out over 7 years. To put it in perspective, over those 7 years, we will pay over $3,000 in interest for a $25,000 car at a 4% interest rate. Auto manufacturers also enjoy the longer tenor because consumers will spend more for their cars because the monthly payments are low.

With all of this in mind, my first point regarding purchasing a car is that we should generally avoid purchasing a new car. There's a huge premium for being the first owner to enjoy the new car smell and brand-new styling. That huge price typically drops by 15% to 20% in value the minute we drive the car off the lot, so we would lose $5,000 if we tried to sell our $25,000 car shortly after we bought it.

There are a few exceptions to buying new. For example, if you have an extremely attractive interest rate and you plan to drive the car until it dies, then you might consider a new car. (Even then, I wouldn't personally do it.) If we do purchase new, we should focus on the sale price and not the monthly payment. The dealership will direct us to the low payment because that makes us less sensitive to the actual price of the vehicle, but we need to focus on the actual deal we're getting on the car, not what the monthly payments are. Also, if we plan on trading in a vehicle upon purchasing the car, then we need to treat the trade-in as a separate transaction.

Let's assume you're doing a trade-in. First, negotiate the price of the car you're purchasing, whether that's a new or used car. Then discuss the dealer's sale price for the trade-in. It might be obvious, but I'll say it anyway: do your research regarding the car before you go to the dealership and don't purchase the car the first time you go to the dealership unless you've already negotiated a deal over the phone in advance. The optimal path is to zero in on a style/manufacturer and search the dealership's inventory online, then connect over the phone to discuss the numbers. Why? It's simply more difficult to say "no" in person.

Do your negotiating over the phone. It's more personal when you're on the lot, and buying a car isn't a personal situation—it's business. That's definitely how the dealership is viewing the transaction. If the make/model you want is popular, then a similar car might be at several dealerships, and conducting the transaction over the phone allows you to easily pit one dealership against another. You don't have to mention the other dealership by name, but saying you're getting an offer from another dealer that's hundreds of dollars less will likely result in the other dealer lowering or at least matching. And don't lie about the pricing! But do take your time when purchasing a car, and do your negotiating over the phone using sales figures and facts that you've already researched online.

LIFE PRO TIP *A quick word on leasing a car – this option is almost always a more expensive choice vs. purchasing a reliable used vehicle. Leasing allows us to exchange the vehicle every couple of years (once the lease expires), but we don't have any ownership of the car. Lease payments are basically paying for the depreciation (decreased value) of the car during the years on the lease (which are referred to as the lease terms). Cars can depreciate 15 – 35% over the initial years, so our lease payments are basically paying the car company for that decreased value. When we turn the car back in after the lease, the dealership will then turn around and sell that car at market value. If the vehicle we lease is worth $25,000 at the start of the lease, then after the lease, the vehicle might be worth $18,000, which is what the dealership will sell the vehicle for. The difference, the $7,000 ($25,000 - $18,000 = $7,000), is what we pay during the time of the lease (through our monthly lease payments), so the dealership is basically having us pay for the decreased value of the vehicle during the lease. Bottom line is that if we have enough disposable income to afford to get a new vehicle every couple of years, then a lease might be for you. For the majority of us starting out, though, we should be looking to purchase a high-quality used vehicle and drive it until it dies.*

Student Loans

We can't have a consumer debt discussion without discussing student loans. Student loans have their own characteristics, with the primary difference being that they are permanent and the seven-year rule around defaulted debt falling off of our credit report isn't applicable. **Student loan debt does not go away.** You may already have a great deal of student loan debt. If that's the case, you might want to consider consolidating your debt into a lower-rate loan. The same principles of paying off more than the minimum payment also apply to student loan debt, so making additional payments is very productive. There are also student loan forgiveness programs that include teaching for 5 years, working for a nonprofit organization, participating in the income-driven repayment (IDR) plan, or serving your country by joining either the military or AmeriCorps. I personally feel that joining the military is a great way to have your college funded, plus serving also gives you the opportunity to see the world. If you have few options other than accruing significant student loans, then military service is a great path to consider. I would have likely gone down this path myself if I had been encouraged to understand this option during my early years.

Mortgages

As I mentioned earlier, not all consumer debt is bad. The one exception that comes to mind is mortgage debt. Real estate is generally an appreciating asset over time, so taking out the right level of debt to purchase a home is a good way to accumulate wealth. The tax code is quite friendly when it comes to real estate and allows homeowners to reduce their taxable income by the amount of interest they pay each year on their mortgage. The practical implication here is that what we pay for our mortgage interest reduces our taxable income. This potentially reduces our tax bracket. We'll talk more about the tax benefits of mortgages in the "How Taxes Work" section, but for now, just understand that we can deduct our mortgage interest payments from our taxable income.

How to Address Consumer Debt

Let's now talk strategically about how we're going to tackle various forms of consumer debt. Generally, we want to take inventory of the interest rates related to each form of debt. Each credit card will have a different rate, so we need to look at our statements or call customer service to find out what those rates are. Same for other forms of debt—if we have a car loan, we need to call the lender and ask what the interest rate is. The interest rate related to our mortgage will likely be the lowest because a significant asset backs the loan. (The house itself is the asset, meaning that if something terrible happened and we defaulted, then the mortgage company would foreclose on the property and sell the home to pay off the loan.) The same is likely true for our car loan—if we default, the car is repossessed and sold to pay off the car loan. Again, this rate is typically lower than what credit card debt carries. Because credit cards aren't backed by assets that can be seized, credit card interest rates are likely going to be higher than any other form of debt. And as I mentioned before, mortgage debt comes with tax benefits. Paying off the home mortgage is typically the last debt we'll pay off.

Once we have identified each of our consumer debts and we know our amounts and interest rates, then we need to rank each credit line by its interest rate. Rather than paying more than the minimum payment on all of our credit cards, we're going to make the minimum payment on all of our credit cards *and* make a larger payment on the credit line that carries the highest interest rate. Once we've paid off the highest-interest rate loan and it has a zero balance, then we move to the second-highest credit card and start making more than the minimum payment on *that* credit card while continuing to make minimum payments on the other cards.

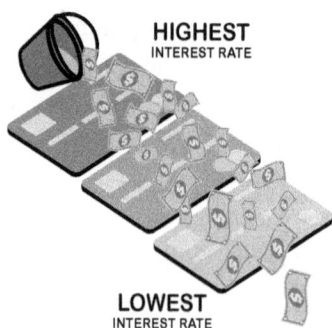

HIGHEST
INTEREST RATE

LOWEST
INTEREST RATE

We'll follow this waterfall approach until we've paid off all of our consumer debts except for maybe our mortgage.

Many people start with the lower-balance credit cards and pay those off first, but the **interest rate is what should drive**

prioritizing which debt we pay off first. We'll start to see a multiplier effect—although the first card will take the longest to pay off, then we'll chip away at the second credit line faster than the first because we're using all the payments that went to the first card we paid off to pay down the second card. Chipping away at the third will go even faster because we're using the payments that we used to pay off the first and second cards to pay off the third. You get the idea—we'll pick up momentum as we pay off each card, going faster and faster until we've paid off all our consumer debts.

Again, our mortgage is different and shouldn't be viewed as "bad" consumer debt. There are strategies we can use to optimize our mortgage debt, including making sure we have a competitive interest rate. If we have a high interest rate on our mortgage, the best path is to refinance, provided that the refinancing rate is lower than our current rate.

How do we know whether we should refinance? First, we should look at the rate we're currently being charged and see if there are any early-repayment penalties. Most mortgages don't have these penalties, but it's best to make sure. Then we want to look at what is currently being offered in terms of interest rates and assess the closing costs and fees related to refinancing. (These are charges the new lending bank will charge us.)

Once we have all of that information, we do the easy math. If the closing fees are, for example, $5,000, then we have to see how many months it takes to make up the $5,000 in fees. The way we're going to make up this $5,000 fee is through the lower rate, which will result in lower-interest payments each month. We'll want to see how much we'll save each month in interest by having a lower rate and see how many months it will take to cover the fees. If we add up the lower interest payments, how many months does it take to get to $5,000? If we plan on living in the house for longer than the number of months it will take to make up the $5,000 in refinancing fees, then yes, refinancing makes economic sense.

REFINANCING FEE OF $5,000 RECOVERED BY YEAR 5

MONTHLY INTEREST PAYMENT DIFFERENCE

	5%			3.50%				
VALUE	$100,000			$100,000				
PERCENTAGE DOWN	20%			20%				
MORTGAGE	$80,000			$80,000				
INTEREST RATE	5%			3.50%				

YEARS AFTER REFINANCED	PAYMENT AMOUNT	5% INTEREST PAID	PRINCIPAL PAID	PAYMENT AMOUNT	3.5% INTEREST PAID	PRINCIPAL PAID	5% INTEREST PAID	3.5% INTEREST PAID	REDUCED INTEREST EXPENSE OVER TIME
YEAR 1	$5,148	$3,973	$1,181	$4,308	$2,775	$1,535	$3,973 - $2,775	= $1,198
YEAR 2	$5,148	$3,913	$1,240	$4,308	$2,721	$1,590	$3,913 - $2,721	= $2,390
YEAR 3	$5,148	$3,849	$1,304	$4,308	$2,664	$1,646	$3,849 - $2,664	= $3,575
YEAR 4	$5,148	$3,783	$1,371	$4,308	$2,606	$1,705	$3,783 - $2,606	= $4,752
YEAR 5	$5,148	$3,714	$1,440	$4,308	$2,545	$1,766	$3,714 - $2,545	= $5,921
YEAR 6	$5,148	$3,639	$1,514	$4,308	$2,482	$1,828	$3,639 - $2,482	= $7,078

Managing consumer debt is something most people don't do well—in fact, racking up consumer debt is what kills most people's chances of ever being financially secure. It's easier to follow the path that most people take and use credit cards for "wants." Don't fall into this trap! If you *are* already in it, you now have a very viable strategy for working your way out over time. It might take years if you have a high balance, but you can do it! Just keep working on maximizing your income, lowering your variable expenses, and using the difference to pay down and eliminate consumer debt.

Step #5 – Investing in IRAs and Other Nontaxable Accounts

Once we've made our 401k contributions up to the employer match and paid down our consumer debt, it's time to focus on other forms of savings. Yes, it may take some time to get to this step, but we will get there eventually! It might not feel realistic right now, but we have to believe that it is possible for us... because it *is*.

In Step #5, we're going to talk about other types of retirement accounts, including 401k accounts and other nontaxable account types. By the way, there are two types of investment accounts: taxable and nontaxable. Taxable accounts aren't linked to retirement savings and include standard brokerage accounts where we might buy stock with money we've saved from our paycheck. However, in this part of the book, we're going to focus on nontaxable accounts. **Nontaxable accounts** are generally related to retirement savings; these accounts are a way for the government to encourage people to set aside funds for later in life. Retirement accounts aren't taxed, hence the name "nontaxable accounts."

Taxable and nontaxable account types can be held at a standard brokerage firm, like Fidelity, Vanguard, or Charles Schwab. There's nothing particularly unique about them.

The nontaxable accounts at brokerage firms are typically referred to as IRA (Individual Retirement Account) accounts. We've already talked about 401k plans, which are administered through our employer. The employer chooses the 401k plan administrator, and we simply sign up for an account through our company's HR department. IRA accounts, on the other hand, typically require *us* to reach out to a brokerage firm and open an account. They're very easy to open and set up for deposits.

There are maximum amounts that the government allows individuals to contribute to their IRA each year. The maximum number typically goes up each year in pace with inflation (more on inflation later in the book). It's very easy to see what the current maximum annual IRA contribution is right now—we can just search "IRA max," and we'll see the current number. There are two types of IRAs: the Roth IRA and the traditional IRA.

A Roth IRA is available for people who have a total taxable income that is below a certain threshold. We can quickly find out what the maximum income is by searching "Roth IRA income." A Roth IRA is a type of savings account where the contributions grow over time on a tax-free basis. If we purchased a mutual fund 2 years ago in our Roth IRA and then sold and purchased another fund, we don't pay taxes on the "capital gains" (the increase in value) of the fund. If we were to execute a similar transaction in a taxable account, then we'd pay taxes on the capital gains from the sale of the mutual fund. But because our contributions to our Roth IRA are made "after tax" (unlike a 401k, which is made before paying taxes), the withdrawals from the Roth at retirement are tax-free.

This means that investments in a Roth IRA grow each year on a tax-free basis, and we aren't taxed when we start taking money out at 59 ½ years of age (or whatever the age limit is when we retire). Remember, our 401k contributions are made before taxes, so while the investments grow tax-free over the years, the withdrawals *are* taxed once you take the money out in retirement. That's not the case for Roth IRAs because our contributions are made with after-tax dollars. Unlike our

401k contributions, we've already paid taxes on our Roth IRA contributions.

The other form of IRA is the traditional IRA. The majority of people can open a Roth IRA, but if our household income is higher than a certain level, then we aren't eligible for a Roth IRA. We can only contribute to a traditional IRA if our income is over the Roth limit. (We can get the latest Roth IRA income levels by searching "Roth IRA income.") Like the Roth IRA, contributions to a traditional IRA are typically made with taxed dollars, and the investments grow tax-free each year. But unlike a Roth IRA, the withdrawals at age 59 ½ are taxed the same way normal income is taxed. To repeat: Roth withdrawals at age 59 ½ *aren't* taxed, but traditional IRA withdrawals *are* taxed at 59 ½.

	401K	ROTH IRA	IRA
CONTRIBUTIONS	NOT TAXED	TAXED	NOT TAXED
WITHDRAWALS	TAXED	NOT TAXED	TAXED
CONTRIBUTIONS LIMITS	$20,500 PER YEAR	$6,000 PER YEAR	
INCOME LIMITS	NONE	UNDER $139,000 (SINGLE) UNDER $206,000 (MARRIED)	HIGHER INCOME LEVELS OVER ROTH IRA LIMTS
WITHDRAWAL AGE LIMIT	59 ½ YEARS OF AGE OR OLDER	ANY TIME	59 ½ YEARS OF AGE OR OLDER
MINIMUM DISTRIBUTION	70 ½ YEARS OF AGE (UNLESS WORKING)	NONE (UNLESS ROTH IRA IS INHERITED)	70 ½ YEARS OF AGE
WHO MAINTAINS THE ACCOUNT?	EMPLOYER	SELF	SELF

There are instances where the traditional IRA can be tax-deductible if our income meets certain thresholds, but we're not going to get into each permutation of how a traditional IRA might be handled. For purposes of this book, we simply want to understand that funding an IRA account is the next bucket we should fill after we've made our 401k company match and paid off our consumer debt. Again, a simple search will identify whether we can contribute to a Roth IRA or a traditional IRA. Particularly if we're starting out early in life, we'll likely be eligible for a Roth IRA. Traditional IRA's are required when your income is in excess of $125k plus so most reading the book will open a Roth IRA. Once it's opened, we can just find a low-cost mutual fund to invest in, like Fidelity's Total Market Index Fund (stock market ticker FSKAX) or Vanguard's Total Market Index Fund (stock market ticker VTSAX). Low-cost mutual funds are defined based on the expense that the fund administrator charges us to invest in the fund. Low-cost funds charge fees that can range from zero to possibly 0.015%, where as some non-indexed funds charge upwards of 0.75% or 1% plus per year in fees. So look at the "Expense Ratio" of the fund you're choosing, which can be found through a simple Google Finance search on the fund name. One more point – if you open a Fidelity account, then buy into Fidelity's Total Market Fund (FSKAX). If you open up a brokerage account with Vanguard, then purchase a Vanguard Total Market Fund (VTSAX). Purchasing the fund that's managed by the broker you choose reduces the fees. Each broker manages and sells a Total Market Fund. The Total Market Fund at each broker is made up of essentially the same group of underlying companies, and it's just the broker managing the fund that's different. Just Google 'Fidelity Total Market Index Fund' or 'Charles Schwab Total Market Index Fund', or 'Vanguard Total Market Index Fund' and you'll easily see which fund to purchase based on the broker you end up opening the account with.

LIFE PRO TIP *Many of us will change employers multiple times throughout our careers, and we'll need to manage our 401k with each move. Once we've left our employer, the 401k plan administrator will likely allow us to keep our investments with them, but it's best to move and consolidate those funds. This is done*

by what's referred to as a "401k rollover into a traditional IRA."
Remember, unlike a Roth IRA, withdrawals from a traditional IRA
in retirement are taxed the same way ordinary income is taxed.
Withdrawals from 401k accounts in retirement are also taxed
as ordinary income. Because both have similar tax implications,
the 401k rollover is best placed into a traditional IRA rollover ac-
count. This is why the 401k can be rolled into the traditional IRA.

Make sure you have the 401k plan administrator with the em-
ployer you're leaving send the funds directly to the traditional
IRA rollover account. Don't take personal possession of the
funds first! That might have tax implications. Follow the simple
rollover instructions at Fidelity or Charles Schwab or whatever
brokerage provider you choose. The broker will certainly be able
to help you with a 401k rollover. You can roll 401k contribu-
tions into the same traditional IRA rollover account each time
you change employers.

Step #6 – Maxing Out Your 401k or Purchasing Income-Producing Assets

We've talked about five steps so far: optimizing your household income statement, establishing an emergency fund, investing in a 401k up to the company match, paying off consumer debt, and contributing to an IRA account to leverage the tax benefits. The last "bucket" that any additional savings should be used for is to purchase income-producing assets, like rental properties or broad market index funds that produce a dividend and also increase in value over time. While the first four steps are pretty straightforward, Steps #5, #6, and #7 are about what to do once you're financially safe and are in a comfortable place with no consumer debt. Getting past the first four steps can take some time, especially Step #4, seeing as most people carry consumer debt. This can take years for some people, but that's okay – we have to start somewhere.

Before we jump into Step #6, we should spend a little more time acknowledging that getting to this stage won't be easy. Like many things in life, getting started is often the hardest part of any journey, and getting past the first four steps will be challenging. You should just acknowledge that and tell yourself that the next 12 to 48 months are going to be tough but that you'll get past them. Those initial steps are what will allow you to reach your goals! Working on financial goals is like working out to get in shape—if you persistently work at it, you will eventually see results. And just like your body becomes more efficient as you get into shape (you'll actually burn more calories throughout the day because your larger muscles will require more energy, so you're burning more calories by just living your normal life), your finances will get more efficient as you get them into shape. That's because, due to interest and appreciation, your money will be working on improving *itself* even when *you're* not working on improving it.

Your money will begin to multiply for you even while you're sleeping if it's invested in assets that grow or produce income. Tell yourself that you're going to put your head down and spend the next 12 to 48 months setting up the rest of your life. Try and get past the first four steps as soon as possible, knowing that they're the hardest steps for sure. During that time, getting a second job is something you should strongly consider. A second job or a side hustle can make a big difference because you'll be earning extra money to pay down consumer debt *and* you'll have less time to spend your income because you'll be working instead of looking for ways to entertain yourself. You can also fast-forward Step #4 (paying down consumer debt) by downsizing your lifestyle and trading in your expensive car with high car payments for an inexpensive yet dependable car. Step #5 allows you to take advantage of non-taxable accounts that provide tax benefits for retirement savings.

Once we've reached Step #6, we should have enough extra income to start investing in non-retirement assets because we're no longer paying down consumer debt. All of those payments that went to consumer debt can now be saved and used to either further contribute to our 401k over and above the company match or invest in things like real estate and other income-producing assets, like broad market index mutual funds.

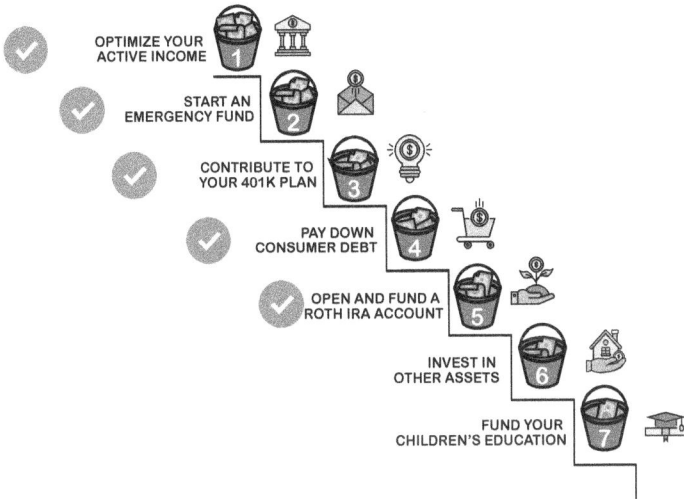

STATUS UPDATE: CONCEPTS DISCUSSED

OPTIMIZE YOUR
ACTIVE INCOME — 1

START AN
EMERGENCY FUND — 2

CONTRIBUTE TO
YOUR 401K PLAN — 3

PAY DOWN
CONSUMER DEBT — 4

OPEN AND FUND A
ROTH IRA ACCOUNT — 5

INVEST IN
OTHER ASSETS — 6

FUND YOUR
CHILDREN'S EDUCATION — 7

In Step #6, maxing out our annual contribution to our 401k account is a very safe and solid approach, but it might not be a good approach for everyone. To be clear, though, we definitely want to save enough to get the company match. Some people decide not to max out their 401k over the company match but rather purchase non-retirement assets like rental properties. Some people may want to use the income from the rentals prior to meeting nontaxable retirement age limits. (Retirement accounts often can't be touched without a penalty until we've reached a minimum age limit, which is often well into our 60s. A simple search for "IRA age limit" or "401k age limit" will give us the latest information as to when we can withdraw from a nontaxable account.)

Some people don't want to wait until reaching the age when the government allows them to retire—they want to control their time and live work-free well before they're eligible to withdraw from retirement accounts. The decision to max out our 401k and IRA versus investing in taxable investments is also based on whether we want to take the more conservative road and max out all retirement savings or take the riskier path with potentially higher rewards by purchasing non-retirement assets. Some people skip Step #5 and want to start investing in assets that aren't encumbered by age withdrawal requirements. I encourage you to think about a life where you're young enough to enjoy an active lifestyle and have a passive income stream that's not related to retirement. This is called being "financially independent." That's having enough income to live off of without working a 9-to-5 job.

The "easiest" asset class to purchase is a broad market index fund with low-cost fees, like VTSAX or FSKAX. Although mutual funds are great and don't require much effort (other than saving the money, which takes a ton of discipline), many have found that purchasing real estate is a more productive approach to tackling Step #6 and often comes with a solid stream of income through rents that are collected monthly. Whatever we choose as our investment vehicle for Step #6, the key takeaway here is that we have options in Step #6.

We know we have to have an emergency fund, and we have to pay off consumer debt. We need to take the free money from our employer and get the employer match. Whether we want to max out other nontaxable accounts (Step #5) is up to each individual. Following all steps, including Step #5, is the safest approach to take, but it's not necessarily the fastest way to financial independence. I've found that real estate is the fastest way. Let's spend some time talking about how real estate investments work, then discuss stocks. We'll finish the Personal Finance section with an overview of the mechanics behind being financially independent.

Life Pro Tip *Conceptualizing the tax implications and benefits can be confusing, but there's a straightforward way to think about this topic. At the end of the day, you have options to contribute to retirement savings based on either a pre-taxed or after-tax basis. The guiding principle should be your view on your current tax rate vs. future tax rate. Chances are, if you're early in your career, you're likely in a lower tax bracket (because your income is likely low), so it's preferable to fund "after-tax" retirement accounts because you're paying the taxes now (with the lower tax bracket) vs. funding "pre-tax" accounts because with "pre-tax" accounts, you're not paying taxes now but will pay taxes later once you withdraw the funds. ROTH IRA account contributions are "after tax," so you're paying the taxes now vs. later which is likely the smarter bet because 1) your income will likely be higher later in life, so your tax rate will be higher, and 2) the tax code can change and taxes will likely go up over time, so you avoid those tax increase if you just fund the ROTH IRA now with after- tax dollars to avoid any future tax burden. This is why many people fund their 401k up to the match using pre-tax dollars up to the company match (so they don't miss out on the match) and then move to fund a ROTH IRA after the company match is completed. Once the ROTH IRA is funded to the max using after-tax dollars, you can go back to the funding the rest of your employers 401k. So fund up to the match, then fund the IRA to the max, and then go back to the 401k and max that out. It comes down to when you want to pay the taxes – now or later. If you fund with pre-tax dollars today, you pay taxes later, but if you fund accounts with after-tax dollars, you're paying the taxes now and avoid any taxes later. Your 401k contributions are pre-tax dollars, and your ROTH IRA contributions are using after tax. If you make too much to qualify for the ROTH IRA, then your only options are all pre-tax – specifically 401k contributions and Traditional IRA contributions. You can only make annual contributions to either a ROTH or a Traditional IRA – not both in the same year.*

Step #7 (Optional) – Funding Your Child's Education

For many readers, this is likely a down-the-road discussion, but funding your potential child's education is an important concept to understand if you want to have a well-rounded understanding of personal finance. Many people view funding their children's education as a primary financial goal. That's great if you can afford to do it! The most common approach is opening up a 529 plan, which allows parents to save for their child's college by participating in a state's 529 plan. The funds can grow tax-free, and the proceeds can be used for college costs at qualified colleges nationwide. Each state has a 529 plan, but we can contribute to any state's plan and then use the proceeds to fund college expenses in any state. We're not tied down to our child going to a specific college or to a college in a specific state.

There are two types of 529 plans: a college savings plan and a prepaid tuition plan. The college savings plan is an account we can contribute to with after-tax dollars. Our investment in that plan grows tax-free (it's very similar to a Roth IRA). Our plan administrator will provide investment options so that our cash contributions grow over time. If the withdrawn funds qualify as education-related, then we aren't taxed on those withdrawn funds.

The other type of 529, the prepaid tuition plan, lets us make after-tax contributions to prepay all or part of a state's in-state college expenses. However, with the prepaid tuition plan, we need to pick the school we want our child to attend. That's because the actual college runs the prepaid tuition plan, whereas the state runs the college savings plan. Prepaid tuition plans also often come with the added benefit of being able to lock in in-state college tuition costs at the start of the plan. This means that our tuition costs will be today's costs even though our child won't be attending college for a while yet. Translation: We won't bear the impact of increased tuition costs as our child grows older over time. Over the last 20 years, tuition costs have outpaced inflation, so locking in today's costs for a child who will go to school 18 years from now is very helpful.

Of course, we never know if our children are going to use their 529 plan. Life happens, and college isn't in the cards for everyone. If a child doesn't have any qualifying education expenses, then when the funds are withdrawn, the investment growth (the capital gains) from the 529 plan is taxed as regular income, plus there is a 10% penalty. The penalty can be waived if the child doesn't use the funds because they received a scholarship or if they avoided college costs by signing up for the military. Death and being disabled are other qualifying factors for avoiding the penalty.

LIFE PRO TIP *Paying for your child's college is nice, but saving for retirement should be a much higher priority. Your child can find ways to pay for school, including smartly managing student loan debt. There is no loan program for retirement! Fund yourself first. The worst-case scenario is that your child takes out loans and you pay them off if you're financially able to do so.*

COLLEGE/TRADE SCHOOLS AND STUDENT LOANS

Everyone has different goals, and traditional college isn't for everyone. That said, if we're in high school and have better-than-average grades and good standardized test results, then taking the next step and going to college is—statistically, at least—one of our better options. If we aren't academically inclined, then maybe college isn't our best option. We still have plenty of paths to take in life, so rather than getting caught in the trap of feeling down about our academic performance, we should focus on succeeding in trades that don't require a four-year degree.

But if you are academically inclined, college should really be on your list of priorities. If you excelled in high school, I encourage you to shoot high in terms of the college you pursue. At the same time, the cost of college should weigh heavily into your decision. If you're eligible for grants or scholarships, then college costs are less relevant, but for those without that kind of financial support, it's important to understand how much your 4 years of college are going to set you back and what your debt will likely be after you graduate.

Too often, students don't assess how their post-college debt will be handled or paid off. Unlike consumer debt (which is discussed elsewhere in this guide), student debt doesn't go away if unpaid. Unfortunately, many times, students pursue a degree, and their job prospects post-college just don't allow for debt repayment plus a fruitful lifestyle. If we do pursue a degree in what's typically a lower-income career, then it's important to consider all options to reduce our student debt before we start taking out loans. One of those is starting at a junior college (also called a community college). Initially, studying at a junior college for 2 years is a very good option—we can obtain an associate degree and then enter a four-year college for our junior and senior years. Attending a community college also often allows us to live at home and further reduce our expenses and lower our student debt. Yes, it's appealing to get out of our parents' houses, but those 2 extra years of living at home and attending community college can mean hundreds of dollars of monthly savings *after* college because we won't be paying back thousands of dollars of student loans.

We should look at the starting salary for our field and how long it typically takes to find a job. What will our career look like in terms of our household income? Will we be able to save while living our choice of lifestyle? If we take out a student loan, what will be our monthly payment? Remember, we'll need to deduct the cost of repaying our student loan repayment from our potential income to see what our net income will be.

For all of these reasons, it's worth looking at other options to pay for school other than student loans. These include but are not limited to enrolling in the military or ROTC, entering a federal job after graduation or becoming a teacher after graduation. We can reduce our student loan debt by teaching for 5 years, working for a nonprofit organization, participating in an income-driven repayment (IDR) plan or serving our country by joining either the military or AmeriCorps.

Many people aren't aware of the IDR option. It basically aligns a federal student loan to the borrower's income, family size, the state in which the borrower lives, and the student loan type. Generally, the IDR plan takes into account the borrower's life situation and makes the repayment amount reflect what's realistically feasible for the borrower. There is a lot of information about IDR plans online, so if you already have student loan debt, do your research.

Also, make sure that the college you're attending isn't a for-profit organization. Often, those types of colleges have the goal of optimizing their income, and that's counter to what you want to accomplish. For-profit schools are also not as respected as not-for-profit schools, and college credits from for-profit schools are sometimes difficult to transfer over to an accredited four-year school. Seek only accredited colleges and avoid for-profit educators.

If academics aren't our strong suit, then attending a trade school is a very good option. In contrast, *not* having a college degree *or* any trade skills will likely result in us having a difficult career. The sooner we acknowledge that fact, the sooner we'll put ourselves on a track to finding success. Waiting around until our 30s to seek training is just a waste of time and will put us further behind in achieving our goals. There will likely always be demand for people who can build and fix homes and infrastructure. Plumbers, electricians, welders, etc, can all often earn salaries well above average. Trade schools are often much less expensive than a four-year college, plus, in many instances, they can result in students getting jobs immediately upon graduation. Being a skilled trades professional provides real career direction.

We need to think of our youth as a time that's foundational to our overall success. Our initial years out of high school can sometimes determine our life's trajectory. If we want the best chance of achieving financial success, then obtaining either a bachelor's degree from an accredited college or a degree from a trade school in a high-demand field are the ways to go. Without one of those things, we'll likely be competing for entry-level jobs that generally don't pay very well. And even though it's entirely possible for our career to start with an entry-level job, we'll likely hit a ceiling with our employer because a degree is typically needed to reach the top of the ladder. A career in a trade likely will allow us to have enough cash flow to save a healthy part of our income in the form of income-producing assets while we're also enjoying a great lifestyle.

FINANCIAL INDEPENDENCE – A NEW WAY OF THINKING ABOUT ASSETS

We've talked about the 7 steps to financial security, and we've talked about different investment options like real estate or investing in broad index mutual funds. Now we can take this information and put together a solid plan that sets us on a path to financial security and success. "Financial success" means something different to each person. It could mean having no consumer debt, or it could mean not having to worry about the cost of guacamole when ordering a burrito. In some cases, financial success could mean being able to use the income from our assets (dividends or rental income, for example) to purchase a new toy.

We can take this idea of using our assets to pay for our desired lifestyle to the next level and reach for the real end game of personal finance: financial independence. Let's dive into exactly how this works. Financial independence (often referred to as FI) is the ability to live the lifestyle we choose using our accumulated revenue-producing assets. Essentially, financial independence allows us to choose how we spend our time.

The term "financial independence" often is followed by the term "retire early"; it's referred to as Financial Independence Retire Early (FIRE). The FIRE philosophy has become immensely popular amongst the personal finance crowd over the past decade. It's a philosophy that's really no more complicated than saving a large enough amount of money (or assets that produce money) to allow us to withdraw a small amount each year to meet our financial needs. Many people can "retire" at a young age (in their 40's or early 50's) once they hit their asset goal, hence the "retire early" part. That said, this concept does not mean that we have to retire in the traditional sense of the word. When we think about it, actual retirement is basically financial independence—it's just that most people must wait until they qualify for Social Security and Medicare in order to have enough income to not have to work. I want you to consider a situation where you don't have to wait around for those income streams in order to leave the workforce.

The concepts we're talking about are not just daydreams! These strategies and ideas are very viable for people who have enough time on their side to allow for compounding interest to do its magic or for those who put the necessary effort into real estate investing. Many readers will feel like these strategies are way out of their grasp, but just because these ideas might not be applicable today doesn't mean we shouldn't consider them to be possibilities for us. All of the strategies in this book are absolutely possible to achieve. It's just a matter of effort and time.

Being financially independent doesn't necessarily mean that we need to retire—we can continue to work *and* be financially independent. The difference is that we don't *have* to work. If we get a new boss who makes our life an absolute nightmare, we can quit and have no concerns about meeting our expenses without a 9-to-5 job. I'm not an advocate for making rash decisions when it comes to employment—it's generally important to have another job lined up before you resign—but financial independence gives you what some people call "FU money." This means having an alternate income stream that allows you to say f*** off to your boss (metaphorically) and not really have to worry about how you're going to pay for your next meal.

Mindset and habits also have a lot to do with the ability to become financially independent. If someone makes $100,000 per year but spends $98,000 per year, they can't walk away from a job they hate. They're shackled to it. They know the job affords them the lifestyle they're accustomed to—keeping the job is critical. They'll never really get out of that cycle because as their income has grown over the years, their lifestyle needs have grown, too, and they haven't delayed gratification enough to accumulate income-producing assets. We talked about this earlier - this is called "lifestyle creep."

If you get a raise, don't spend it! Instead, increase your monthly savings by that amount. Don't go buy a nicer car that comes with a higher monthly payment just because your income went up. Save the difference and remember the difference between "needs" and "wants." Many people who spend mostly on wants give the appearance of being wealthy without actually having any real net worth.

Let's now transition to the fundamentals of financial independence. As we've already discussed, we can achieve FI by developing enough income-producing assets to pay for our chosen lifestyle. Often, that lifestyle comes after the asset-accumulation phase of our lives, a time when we're executing the 7 steps. Making regular contributions to our savings or accumulating assets can take years or decades, depending on our income level and the cost of our chosen lifestyle.

Many people live a much thinner lifestyle during their asset-accumulation phase than what they aspire to live once they have achieved financial independence. There is, of course, a balance here—we must live our lives and enjoy every day. The journey we're making to get to our goals *is* our life, so we shouldn't make our lives absolutely miserable by depriving ourselves of any joy that is accompanied by an expense. We will, though, need to delay buying material items that would otherwise use up cash we should be plowing into our savings.

So far, we've focused on two types of investments once we've hit Step #6: stocks (primarily mutual funds) and real estate. Although there are countless types of assets, these two asset classes attract the average retail investor.

Where our assets are invested has a lot to do with what interests us and whether we want to have a totally hands-off approach to investing. As I've mentioned, the "easiest" form of investing might not be the fastest path to a high net worth, but it is the most hands-off and requires the least amount of investor know-how and ongoing maintenance. That would be investing in a simple broad market index mutual fund with low fees. Many people in the personal finance space recommend a total market index fund like Vanguard's VTSAX or Fidelity's FSKAX fund (same fund basket but with different brokers). Both funds have very low costs (fees) and do a good job of diversifying the companies that the funds are invested in.

That said, these funds aren't for everybody. The more familiar you become with various stocks and mutual fund options, the more you can customize your investment strategy. In broad strokes, though, a non-brainer investment option that spreads out risk across the whole market is either of those two mutual funds. A more tangible, hands-on approach to investing is in real estate. We'll spend some time in the next chapter discussing the actual income streams that come from both of these investment types.

By now, I hope you have a sense of how you can develop your financial plan by using the 7 steps. Once we've reached Step #6 and have been saving for years, we might find that we've contributed a great deal to retirement accounts that are restricted until we reach a certain minimum age. Step #6 is all about building assets that are not necessarily retirement-related. However, we're still building our nontaxable accounts over the years as we follow Step #3 (401k employer match) and Step #5 (further contributing to nontaxable accounts).

If we do want to retire early once we've accumulated enough assets, we might run into a tax challenge due to the age penalty imposed on withdrawals from nontaxable accounts before a certain age. This might make the RE ("retire early") part of the FIRE philosophy hard because we aren't old enough to touch the funds in a 401k or an IRA without paying a penalty. Remember, the IRS imposes a 10% penalty for individuals who withdraw from nontaxable accounts if they're below a certain retirement age. Some people might have hundreds of thousands of dollars in their 401k or IRA but can't touch it because they're too young.

Other options do address this situation, including either a Roth conversion ladder or what's referred to as "Rule 72T" (related to Tax Code 72(T), section 2). These tax-friendly solutions allow individuals to convert nontaxable accounts (401ks, IRAs) into taxable accounts, which can then be withdrawn from without incurring the 10% minimum-age-related penalty. There are specific requirements around planned withdrawals over a five-year period where the individual maps out the conversion of the 401k or IRA funds into five tranches of equal value. One tranche is then withdrawn per year over a five-year period. The individual will pay ordinary income taxes on each of the five withdrawals, but they won't be penalized 10% for early withdrawal. Remember, 401k contributions are made before taxes, so it's only fair that the individual pays ordinary income taxes when the funds are actually withdrawn.

Because these solutions can be complicated, we won't go into too much depth about them here. But it's important for us to understand that we have options to access our retirement accounts if we decide to pull the trigger on the RE part of the FIRE philosophy. I strongly encourage you to engage with an accountant if you're seriously considering this option. There is plenty of information on this topic in the public domain, though, if you want to get smarter regarding your options for accessing retirement accounts prior to the IRS age requirement.

LIFE PRO TIP *Chances are, there are investing clubs in your area with similarly-minded individuals who are interested in personal finance. Find out where these clubs meet and start to network. This is where you can develop a team who can be a sounding board for questions and ideas. If you don't have access to a physical group, then go online and play an active role in real estate investing or personal finance groups. The idea here is to have ongoing dialog with people who are ahead of you in the game so that you can learn from others. That will give you the confidence you need to have a command of your options in Step #6.*

The Mechanics of Saving and Building Assets

I think a lot of people—particularly younger people—don't prioritize saving because it's sometimes hard to have a vision for the future. There are few short-term benefits to saving, and it's much more "fun" to go out and spend now. Retirement is viewed as an event that occurs in our 60s, and that can be 40+ years away for many readers. "Way too far away to worry about it right now!" is the typical mindset. But developing a lifestyle where living below our means and investing to reach a financial goal makes saving today more tangible. Understanding the bigger picture allows us to push to grow our balance sheet. Retirement is one component of our plan, but having a more disciplined approach to spending gives us many other benefits, too! It's best to have a purposeful approach rather than just look at our paycheck and think about how much money we have to spend on wants rather than just needs.

Another reason why people do not save is that they may already have a great deal of debt and simply don't want to address the problem. They think that saving doesn't really matter because they'll never get out of their consumer debt. Avoiding the subject is easier than developing a plan. Not having a solid understanding of our personal finances and not having a plan and goals makes saving for the future boring. But if we have an end game in mind—like owning passive income-producing rentals or having a significant amount of cash in a broad index fund—then the journey becomes part of the goal. Every time we save just a little, we're chipping away at a goal that's not just financial security but eventual freedom through financial independence (either before or at retirement age).

It's perfectly fine to have little savings and no understanding of what it takes to become financially free. However, that kind of lifestyle requires that we continue to work to pay off debt that continues to grow with no end in sight. Many people have simply fallen into the debt trap without really knowing what they're getting themselves into. They see their friends and family spending freely, and because they want to show that they are also "successful," they pay for that appearance with consumer debt. It's much better to understand the dynamics that underpin financial success and make the conscious and pointed decision to spend wisely.

When we understand these dynamics and commit to spending time building our assets, we'll become financially independent and be able to live off our assets without the need for additional active income that comes from a 9-to-5 job. That said, financial independence does not necessarily mean retirement—at least, not retirement in the traditional sense. Often, people who are financially independent continue to work because humans need tasks to solve, and many people find joy in their careers. Solving problems, working with people we like and engaging with clients are all reasons why people continue to work after having achieved financial independence.

Being FI *does* mean that we don't have to work for a boss we don't get along with. It *does* mean we won't be financially stressed if our employer suddenly closes their business or our role is eliminated. Being FI affords us the ability to *choose* to work. Our job is less stressful when we don't have to worry about the ramifications should we lose it. FI gives us options: we can continue working in our field for the same employer, we can retire early and pursue leisurely pursuits, or we can leave our primary field and find work in a field that interests us. FI can be anything we want it to be.

The 4% Rule

Within the FI community, there's a common agreement as to how to achieve FI. It's centered around the Trinity Study, also referred to as the "4% rule." The Trinity Study took place in 1998 and was conducted by three professors of finance at Trinity University. The study looked at the returns for a portfolio made up of stocks and bonds and mapped out historical (actual) returns from 1925 to 1995. It concluded that an individual has a 96% chance of not running out of money over a 30-year period if funds are withdrawn from the individual's portfolio at an annual 4% rate. At its core, the study attempted to determine a "safe withdrawal rate" (SWR) from a portfolio of stocks and bonds with the goal of not running out of money over a certain period of time. Basically, the SWR is the percentage of funds you can take out of your investments that will allow you to have your money last for at least 30 years. If you have, say, $500,000 in stock and bonds, you can safely withdraw $20,000 per year and have a 96% chance of not running out of money for 30 years. If you reduce the SWR to 3.5%, the chance of running out of money is nearly zero—you can withdrawal $17,500 annually from your $500,000 and have a nearly 100% chance of never running out of money.

How does this work? Over the last 95 years, the stock market has grown at a rate of 7% to 8% in annual returns on average. Yes, the market will have years when the returns are negative (meaning the portfolio loses value), and there will also be years when the stock market is up by double digits. On average, though, over an extended period of time, the market will increase by 7% to 8%. So if you withdraw 4% from your portfolio, then you're leaving 3% to 4% of it to grow (7% to 8% minus 4% SWR = 3% to 4%). Why do you need to keep 3% to 4% left over each year? One word: inflation.

Economists refer to inflation as being "too many dollars chasing too few goods." This means that as more and more people have access to more cash, the prices of goods will eventually go up because the free market will increase pricing. Then demand goes down because the goods in question have increased in price. The supply of money plays a key role in inflation—as more dollars circulate in the system, people will eventually have more dollars in their checking accounts, meaning they will put pressure on goods because they have money to purchase them. Manufacturers will find a new price point that allows them to maximize their revenue and increase the price; eventually, the demand for the product will go down. But that higher price is attractive to people who really want the product.

All of that is why inflation results in the prices of products going up. Over time, inflation in the US has averaged about 2.5%, meaning that the prices of consumer goods go up by 2.5% per year on average. That means the gallon of milk purchased for $4 this year will likely cost $4.10 one year from now. This adds up over time—inflation almost doubled the price of the average consumer good between 1990 and 2020. So if you only withdraw 4% as your SWR, you're left with 3% to 4% because the market in-

7% - **4%** = **3%**
INFLATION   SWR   HANDLING INFLATION

creases by 7% to 8% on average (7% average return minus 4% SWR = 3%). The 3% will allow your assets to grow at the average rate of inflation (again, historically 2.5%) so that your money grows at pace with inflation. If we didn't solve for inflation, we'd eventually run out of money because prices will continue to go up, and we wouldn't have saved the 3% each year, which handles inflation. Without accounting for that reality, our investments wouldn't increase to offset those price increases.

A simplified (or reverse) approach to this rule is to develop our budget for the lifestyle we want to live and multiply that by 25. The times-25 approach is simply the 4% rule reverse-engineered, where 4% x 25 = 100%. For example, let's say our lifestyle requires an annual budget of $60,000. The shortcut math is $60,000 x 25 = $1,500,000 in a portfolio of stocks and bonds. The reverse math is $1,500,000 x 4% = $60,000.

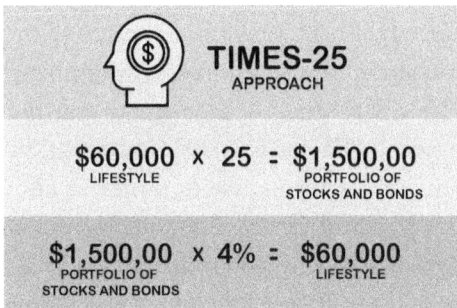

TIMES-25 APPROACH

$60,000 x 25 = **$1,500,00**
LIFESTYLE   PORTFOLIO OF
STOCKS AND BONDS

$1,500,00 x 4% = **$60,000**
PORTFOLIO OF   LIFESTYLE
STOCKS AND BONDS

Using the $60,000 per year lifestyle spend, in Year 1 of deducting from our portfolio, we'll take out $60,000. The next year we will account for inflation, so next year's lifestyle spend will be $60,000 x 3% inflation = $61,800. Because we're deducting our portfolio by 4% and leaving the remaining 3% to handle inflation, we can increase our withdrawal to account for inflation. Our baseline withdrawal is $60,000, but we increase that amount every year by 3% so that we can purchase the gallon of milk that might cost $5 (up from $4) in the next 10 years. Our lifestyle won't need to go down because inflation is making goods more expensive—we can have the same quality of life that the $60,000 gave us in the first year of withdrawing from our portfolio because we're increasing the $60,000 amount each year to account for inflation.

Again, the journey to FI takes time. Over time, as I deposit small amounts into my brokerage account, I'll think about how that contribution will pay for monthly expenses one day. If I deposit $2,500 into my account, I'll think about how the $2,500 will one day allow me to deduct $100 per year until the end of my life ($2,500 x 4% = $100). And that's if I start deducting today. If my FI goal horizon is 10 years down the road and if I make just the average return on my investment, then that $2,500 should double over the 10 years up to over $5,000. That means I'll be able to deduct a little over $200 per year or $16.66 per month. The $2,500 investment will pay for my monthly streaming service for the rest of my life!

Doing the math here also allows us to consider how many more years we might have to work as we spend money. That's particularly meaningful when thinking about big-ticket items. Let's say we have the option of buying a 6-year-old Honda for $10,000 or a new BMW for $35,000. If we take out a five-year auto loan with a 5% interest rate to purchase either car, we'll end up paying $11,300 for the $10,000 Honda and $39,600 for the $35,000 BMW. The difference between the two cars is $28,300 over 5 years. If the difference ($660 monthly for the BMW minus $189 for the Honda = $471) each month is deposited into a brokerage account and invested over the 5 years, we'll have nearly $30,000 in savings. That will produce $1,200 per year in passive income one day ($30,000 x 4% SWR). If we invest that $30,000 for the next 10 years, then it should grow to around $60,000, which is $2,400 per year in passive income ($60,000 x 4% = $2,400) or $200 per month. Buying the Honda versus the BMW leaves us with $200 per month in passive income until we die, while purchasing the BMW versus the Honda doesn't produce the $200 per year in 10 years—rather, it leaves us with a used BMW that will continue to depreciate in value. The Honda would likely still be fine for everyday use.

TOTAL ASSETS (JANUARY 1ST)	ASSET GROWTH THROUGHOUT THE YEAR (@ 7%)	TOTAL WITHDRAWALS THROUGHOUT THE YEAR (4% SWR)	TOTAL ASSETS (DECEMBER 31ST)
FIRST YEAR	$ 1,500,000.00	+ $ 105,000.00	- $ 60,000.00	= $ 1,545,000.00
SECOND YEAR	$ 1,545,000.00	+ $ 108,150.00	- $ 61,800.00	= $ 1,591,350.00
THIRD YEAR	$ 1,591,350.00	+ $ 111,394.50	- $ 63,654.00	= $ 1,639,090.50
FOURTH YEAR	$ 1,639,090.50	+ $ 114,736.34	- $ 65,563.62	= $ 1,688,263.22
FIFTH YEAR	$ 1,688,263.22	+ $ 118,178.43	- $ 67,530.53	= $ 1,738,911.11

AMOUNT SAVED (TOTAL ASSETS) $ 1,500,000.00

ANNUAL SWR   4%

ANNUAL INFLATION (AVERAGE)   3%

ANNUAL INVESTMENT GAIN (AVERAGE)   7%

"DECREASE IN SPENDING VAUE DUE TO INFLATION"
IS OFFSET BY "BALANCE GROWTH PER YEAR" SO SPENDING POWER REMAINS FLAT

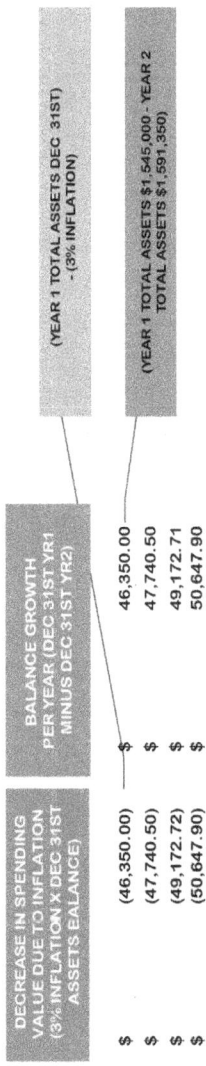

DECREASE IN SPENDING VALUE DUE TO INFLATION (3% INFLATION X DEC 31ST ASSETS EALANCE)	BALANCE GROWTH PER YEAR (DEC 31ST YR1 MINUS DEC 31ST YR2)	(YEAR 1 TOTAL ASSETS DEC 31ST) - (3% INFLATION)
$ (46,350.00)	$ 46,350.00	(YEAR 1 TOTAL ASSETS $1,545,000 - YEAR 2 TOTAL ASSETS $1,591,350)
$ (47,740.50)	$ 47,740.50	
$ (49,172.72)	$ 49,172.71	
$ (50,647.90)	$ 50,647.90	

Making the choice to purchase a good, reliable, used car rather than a new one is a much more efficient use of our money and produces a materially better outcome years after the purchase.

	$2,500 INITIAL INVESTMENT				8% ANNUAL INVESTMENT RETURN
YEARS INVESTED	ACCOUNT BALANCE/GROWTH				ANNUAL INCOME
	$2,500	X	4%	=	$100
YEAR 1	$2,700	X	4%	=	$108
YEAR 2	$2,916	X	4%	=	$117
YEAR 3	$3,149	X	4%	=	$126
YEAR 4	$3,401	X	4%	=	$136
YEAR 5	$3,673	X	4%	=	$147
YEAR 6	$3,967	X	4%	=	$159
YEAR 7	$4,285	X	4%	=	$171
YEAR 8	$4,627	X	4%	=	$185
YEAR 9	$4,998	X	4%	=	$200
YEAR 10	$5,397	X	4%	=	$216

Making the right financial decisions early on makes all the difference later in life. Despite this, the vast majority of people focus only on monthly payments when they think about consumer debt and don't consider the long-term effects of making poor financial decisions. Poor financial decisions are quite easy to identify: if we can't afford to pay for something with cash (meaning we're not incurring debt with the transaction), then it's likely not something we should be buying. Larger purchases such as a car will sometimes require financing, but generally, it's really not a good idea to use financing unless it's absolutely necessary. (Although again, a mortgage is a different situation.) We can strategically use credit cards for points instead of using cash, but it's important to be able to pay off the credit card in full at the end of the month.

	NEW BMW	6-YEAR-OLD HONDA	
	$35,000	**$10,000**	

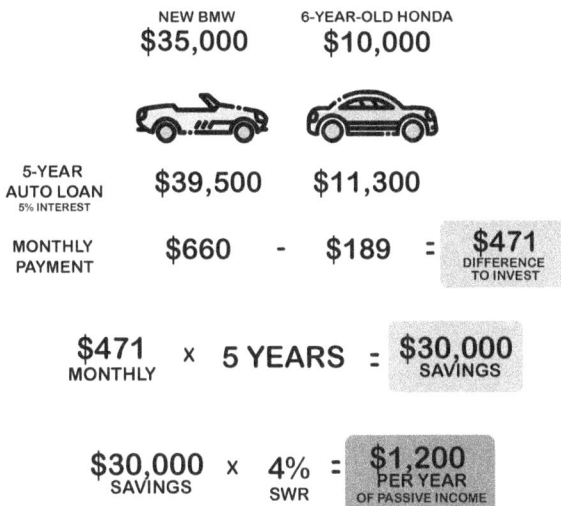

| 5-YEAR AUTO LOAN 5% INTEREST | **$39,500** | **$11,300** | |
| MONTHLY PAYMENT | **$660** - | **$189** = | **$471** DIFFERENCE TO INVEST |

$471 MONTHLY x **5 YEARS** = **$30,000** SAVINGS

$30,000 SAVINGS x **4%** SWR = **$1,200** PER YEAR OF PASSIVE INCOME

The timeline to achieve financial independence really depends on our savings rate and the amount of money we spend. Some people are perfectly fine with living a very minimalistic lifestyle—they can happily live on $15,000 to $20,000 per year. This is certainly possible in some areas of the country, especially if we enjoy cooking and have low-cost hobbies. We can purchase a used electric car and save a lot on gas; we can purchase Amazon basics or gently used clothing and household goods. Many people who can happily live on less make the decision to purchase a very small home in a low-cost-of-living location and either pay cash for the home or know they will be able to pay it off quickly. Then they can easily live off $1,500 per month, which would require $450,000 in income-producing assets. That sounds like a lot of money, but if you are diligent and save $500 on average per month starting at age 20, you'd have about $450,000 by the time you're 45. (That's assuming a very conservative way of investing through mutual funds. Many people develop investments in long-term rental properties, and income from rent provides much more than the $1,500 that's necessary in my example.)

So how do we save $500 per month? Well, we can cut down on our expenses and only purchase needed items, thus minimizing our wants. Or we can do everything possible to maximize our earnings. I personally wanted to have a more comfortable lifestyle, so earning more money was my strategy. I laid a foundation that enabled me to earn an income that gave me the means to live the lifestyle I wanted and *also* save money.

Early in my career, I worked a full-time job at a customer service center *and* worked a second job in the evenings and on weekends. That way, I could live the lifestyle I wanted but also had enough left over to save. Working a second job not only provides more income, but it also reduces the free time we have to spend money. I used to say to myself that if I worked enough hours, I could afford to do what I wanted in my free time because I'd have more money *and* less free time to spend it. We use the term "side hustle" these days, but it really just means finding other ways to bring in income. When I was in college, for example, I was able to live the lifestyle I wanted by bartending, working as a telemarketer, and selling marketing merchandise to fraternities and sororities. Looking back now, that all seems daunting, but at the time, I just put my head down and did it. But I wouldn't recommend doing all of that to you because if you're in school or considering going back to school, getting good grades and finishing school should be your priority. I was actually gambling with my future. Finishing college (or trade school) enables you to have a career and maximize your earning potential.

After graduating from college, though, part-time jobs will always be available to people who are willing to do them. Some won't be fun, like the telemarketing job I had where I was told "No" about 100 times over a four-hour period and maybe got 6 or 7 "Yes" responses a day. Still, I toughed out a good 3 years there so that I could save more and invest more while living the lifestyle I wanted. As we're putting in these kinds of efforts, we'll continue to develop the potential of our full-time job over time, and if we're not falling into the lifestyle creep pattern, then we should be able to save more and more. Eventually, we won't need the part-time job because we'll be on a good path with our full-time job.

Saving to reach FI asset goals takes a long time. We often need to put in 15, 20, or 25 years of effort while focusing on saving cash and not living beyond our means. It does indeed require a great deal of cost management and finding ways to increase our net income. Finding a good side hustle is important and can fast-forward our FI path by many years.

Early in my career, I also found that being flexible with where I lived made a huge difference in how quickly I moved up the ranks with my employer. I frequently looked at internal job postings and raised my hand for a role in another state. Out of college, I lived in six different cities over an eight-year period and followed career opportunities with every move. Everyone's personal situation is different, of course, but if you can, be flexible and open to changes like that.

As already stated, having a lower spend per year makes attaining FI much easier. Some people take their FI dreams to an extreme and live in converted vehicles, surviving on a couple of hundred dollars per month. While this lifestyle isn't for me, it can be great for those who value their free time more than having material possessions. If you can live on $1,000 per month, that's "only" $300,000 in net worth ($300,000 X 4% SWR). Let's say you've earned a degree or learned a trade in a very financially prudent way and you walk away from school with a minimal amount of student debt. Let's also assume you're making $60,000 per year or $45,000 after taxes. That's about $3,750 per month after taxes. If you're spending $1,000 per month, then you're left with $2,750 per month. It would take about 9 years to save $300,000 (assuming an 8% rate of return). Although the math is easy, the effort won't be. But if you continue to only need $1,000 per month to live, then you can quit working after 9 years. Now you should recognize that inflation will play a role over those 9 years, so your $1,000 per month in today's dollars will be worth less 9 years from now. You will likely need to have closer to $350,000 saved in 9 years (due to inflation), but you get the point. That might lengthen the number of years of work to closer to 10 years, but if your income increases over that time, so should the $2,750 per month you're saving. If your savings amount increases from the starting $2,750, then that will shorten the number of years required to reach your net worth goal.

The question is, are you willing to go to extremes to live independently? Some people are perfectly fine living very lean. Just remember: the lower your monthly spend is, the quicker you can achieve financial independence. That's for two reasons. One is because your annual spend is low, you can save a lot per month while you're working, and the second reason is because your annual spend is so low that saving the annual spend times 25 is achievable over a relatively short period of time.

FRUGAL LIVING
MAXIMIZING SAVINGS AT AN EARLY AGE

8% INVESTMENT RETURN

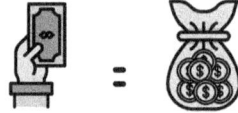

YEARS INVESTED	ANNUAL INCOME		ANNUAL SPEND		ANNUAL SAVED	ACCUMULATED SAVED	ANNUAL INCOME (SWR 4%)
YEAR 1 (12 MONTHS)	$45,000	-	$12,000	=	$33,000	$33,000	$1,320
YEAR 2 (24 MONTHS)	$45,000	-	$12,000	=	$33,000	$68,640	$2,746
YEAR 3 (36 MONTHS)	$45,000	-	$12,000	=	$33,000	$104,280	$4,171
YEAR 4 (48 MONTHS)	$45,000	-	$12,000	=	$33,000	$139,920	$5,597
YEAR 5 (60 MONTHS)	$45,000	-	$12,000	=	$33,000	$175,560	$7,022
YEAR 6 (72 MONTHS)	$45,000	-	$12,000	=	$33,000	$211,200	$8,448
YEAR 7 (84 MONTHS)	$45,000	-	$12,000	=	$33,000	$246,840	$9,874
YEAR 8 (96 MONTHS)	$45,000	-	$12,000	=	$33,000	$282,480	$11,299
YEAR 9 (108 MONTHS)	$45,000	-	$12,000	=	$33,000	$318,120	$12,725
YEAR 10 (120 MONTHS)	$45,000	-	$12,000	=	$33,000	$353,760	$14,150

We've already discussed how we should think about our personal balance sheet. We've accounted for our assets and liabilities, which results in our net worth. In that walk-through, we included our primary residence in the Assets column. Opinions vary as to whether we should do that. Some argue that assets need to be income-producing (like stocks and rentals) or assets that can eventually be sold for a profit (like gold and land). This view needs to be considered when developing our net worth requirements for being financially independent. In the context of being FI, we should only look at assets that create passive streams of income when developing our net worth goal. It's fine to include our home equity, but we obviously can't include that number when looking at whether we have enough income-producing assets to leave the workforce because our home won't produce income to spend. (If we sell it, we'll need to find somewhere else to live.) That said, our annual spend will be lower if we own our home, so there's a clear benefit despite how it's handled on our balance sheet.

Let's spend a minute talking about the details of developing our required income to be financially independent. We'll need to look at our balance sheet and start by adding up the amount of cash we have in stocks and bonds. We can use the 4% SWR rule for cash that's invested in these assets. If we have real estate in our balances, we need to forecast our annual net income from rents and then add that to the 4% SWR proceeds generated by the stocks and bonds we might also own. We might also have other income streams stemming from other sources, like small business investments or income from a website.

We just need to add up all of our various income streams to get to our annual passive income amount. Once we've reached passive income streams that are greater than the cost of our lifestyle, then we've reached FI. That's why many people don't include their home in their balance sheet—a home doesn't produce income. But again, living in a paid-off home saves us a lot of money, so our living expenses go down, and so does the amount we need to save to reach our FI goals. To be clear, owning a home is typically the best way to grow our wealth over time – it's how the majority of households hold their wealth.

Whether we decide to include our home equity or not, the important takeaway is that we need to look at only our income-producing assets when coming up with our annual passive income stream. The times-25 rule is just that: a quick way of thinking about what our net worth needs to be in order for us to reach our FI goal by using stocks and bonds. Stocks and bonds produce both dividends and capital gains (stock appreciation) over time. Dividends are the proceeds that shareholders get when the company disperses its net income to its owners (the shareholders). This is why we can deduct 4% from those investments per year via the SWR—the combination of dividends and capital gains is what makes up the average market returns of 7% to 8%.

I'll wrap up the financial independence discussion by again pointing out that although money isn't the most important thing in life, with money comes options. Each dollar saved provides some type of option. If we've saved for 25+ years, then our assets might provide options that allow us to spend our time the way we want to spend it. Those assets might give us the option to work in a different field that we love, but that might pay less. Having money isn't everything, but if we *don't* have money, then it's typically a constant source of stress. I've lived life without money and I've lived life with money, and I can tell you that life is easier when accompanied by financial success and security. Life is more complicated if we have to worry about the things that money can solve, like how we're going to fix our car or the leak in our roof or whether we can pay our phone bill.

It's true that money can't buy happiness—significant wealth levels that exceed our needs and wants have diminishing returns on happiness. But that doesn't mean that people who struggle with money should learn to be content without the security that money provides in terms of basic necessities and financial security. Sure, money can introduce problems if we're not careful, but I'd much rather manage the problems related to having too much money than the challenges related to barely getting by financially. It's true that having money doesn't result in automatically being happy. Whether we're happy or not typically comes down to the differences between our expectations and our reality. Money just makes it easier to create the reality we want.

LIFE PRO TIP *It can be tempting to share your financial success with friends and family, but generally speaking, it's not a good idea to openly share your financial situation, especially the specific numbers. Often times, sharing results in family or friends asking for financial assistance. It can also result in others feeling animosity toward your success. It's fine if you want to share that you have financial goals and that you're focusing on your future, but I would avoid going into the details. Keep your numbers to yourself to avoid difficult situations. If you want to provide financial assistance to friends and family, treat that assistance as a gift and don't expect to be paid back. Loaning money to close acquaintances rarely plays out well. Gift the money and don't look back or bring it up again.*

Real Estate Investments

Investing in real estate isn't a get-rich-quick approach to building financial independence—it takes time to get *into* real estate and it takes time to get *out* of real estate. But I'm sharing the basics so that you can view investing in real estate as one of your options.

A lot of us feel that real estate investing is either extremely complicated or impossible because we think we have to be rich to get into it. That's just not true—real estate investing is possible for any of us if we take the time to understand the mechanics and think through the right strategy that works for us. I myself didn't have the funds to get to Step #6 until well into my 30s. While the topic of real estate might not be relevant if you're reading this book right out of school, as I've mentioned before, the topics we're covering are meant to be foundational for life. It's important to understand these concepts for down the road, when you will be in a position to take advantage of these types of opportunities. Think of this book as your Advanced Placement course for financial independence!

If you don't consider these options, then they will never be in your future.

The number one reason most people get into real estate is because it's one of the most effective ways to develop passive income. This can be an important tool to improve our personal balance sheet! There are many different real estate strategies (and many resources about real estate investing), but the two most relevant strategies for individual investors are 1) buy and hold or 2) buy and flip. We're not going to explore all the various angles of real estate investments, but we will explore some of what's available to you so that you can start to look at this kind of investing as a very real possibility.

Buy and Hold

Let's start with buying and holding real estate. It's much like it sounds: we find the right real estate deal, make the necessary modifications to get the real estate rent-ready, and then rent it out. I like the buy-and-hold strategy because it offers two benefits: 1) over time, the asset will appreciate in value and can be sold for a profit at a later date, and 2) we will have a passive income stream through collecting rent from our tenants.

Finding the right deal is what's most important here, because the real money in real estate happens when the asset is purchased. That means that the right deal can generate immediate equity. Equity, in this context, is the value of the home versus what we bought it for. If we purchased the home for $75,000 and then made $10,000 in improvements, we would have $85,000 invested into the home. If those improvements then allow us to then sell the home for, say, $100,000, then we would have $15,000 in equity ($100,000 in value minus $85,000 in cash investments).

You may have heard the phrase, "This home has good bones." This means that while there is likely a great deal of cosmetic work that needs to be done (new floors, repainting, bathroom updates, etc.), the foundation is solid. The roof might need to be replaced, but it's structurally sound. Buy-and-hold investors focus on purchasing homes that need work on the key areas of the home that have the highest returns on investment. These updates typically focus on the kitchen, bathroom(s), flooring, paint, and yard. The rehab might be more extensive and include a new roof or a change in the floorplan, but a typical rehab is more cosmetic in nature.

Finding properties that require rehabilitation is the typical path for many real estate investors because these distressed properties can be purchased below market value—most people who are house hunting want a home that is move-in ready. Many don't have the vision or funds to imagine the future home once all the renovations have been completed, or they don't want to get tied up in remodeling because they feel they don't know enough about the process and don't want to deal with the hassle.

When buyers find a "good-bones" home, they can invest in rehabbing the home to get it into proper rental condition, renting out the property and refinancing the property to get their initial investment back. Then buy-and-hold investors can find the next home in need of repair and do the same thing all over again. The key step here is the value that's created at the purchase and rehab stages. If it's done right, that value will allow the investor to take out a mortgage on the property that's equal to the amount of cash invested. That way, the investor basically gets their initial invested cash out of the investment (through bank financing), allowing them to use the same cash they used to purchase the house to then purchase the next investment property…which will then be rehabbed, rented out, and refinanced. Ditto for the next property and the next one. The renter pays the mortgage payments plus other ongoing costs via the monthly rent, and the owner (the landlord) has a monthly income stream of whatever's left. These deals happen every day and in just about every market. All it takes is the time and effort to find the right deal.

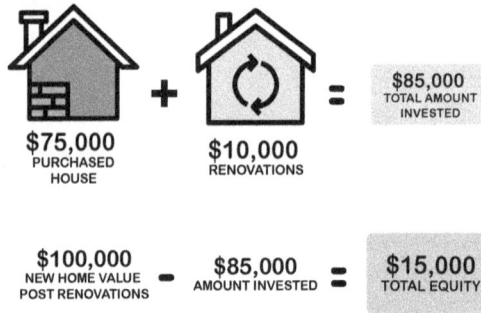

$75,000
PURCHASED
HOUSE

+

$10,000
RENOVATIONS

=

$85,000
TOTAL AMOUNT
INVESTED

$100,000
NEW HOME VALUE
POST RENOVATIONS

−

$85,000
AMOUNT INVESTED

=

$15,000
TOTAL EQUITY

Yes, buying real estate can be a scary thing—but it shouldn't be. Real estate is one of the few assets that are tangible. Not only that, it can be a very fun process to get involved in. It's a great feeling to know that you own land and are providing shelter for others in the community. We just have to read the real estate market and avoid purchasing when it's a "seller's market." A seller's market means that the sellers have the advantage. Often, that's because there's a low inventory of homes or because mortgage interest rates are low, enabling buyers to finance a higher purchase price because their monthly interest payments (the "I" in "P&I") are lower, and therefore, the principal amount can be higher.

Buyers are typically worried more about the monthly payment versus the total price of the home, which is actually the wrong way of thinking. It's just like buying a car. Don't get distracted by the low monthly payments—instead, make sure the price of the home or car is competitive. In a seller's market, the prices of homes go up, and often times, buyers have to compete with each other and make bids in a situation where the highest bid will be accepted. This is sometimes referred to as a "bidding war." We know when real estate is a seller's market, because it typically generates a lot of news.

I generally recommend avoiding purchasing properties during a seller's market. We have to get a good deal on our initial investment, and bidding wars often don't allow for that. In contrast, in a *buyer's* market, the housing inventory is high, and sellers are working hard to sell their properties. High interest rates might be making people reluctant to take out a loan due to the high-interest payments they'll have to make. It's essentially the opposite of a seller's market.

But just like seller's markets, buyer's markets are what's referred to as "cyclical," meaning that these dynamics change. A couple of months or years can go by with one type of market, and then the real estate landscape shifts to being the other. We have to be patient and not let emotions play a role when purchasing rental property. If we're currently in a seller's market, we either need to be very careful about our purchases, or we need to hold tight for the market to switch to a buyer's market. "Patience" is the key word here.

We need to consider some other aspects as we think about getting into real estate. If we choose the buy-and-hold approach to real estate investing, we have to decide whether we want to manage our ongoing engagement with renters ourselves or outsource that engagement to a property manager. I personally choose to outsource. That's where the property manager markets the property, conducts all of the necessary background checks on the applicants, executes all the lease documents, and deals with ongoing maintenance issues (broken air conditioners, leaky dishwashers, etc.).

Being a landlord can be a full-time job! It can take away from our ability to maintain our day job and can discourage us from staying hungry to find the next deal because we're down in the weeds of the properties we already own. Property managers typically charge 10% of the monthly rent plus fees for new leases. Property managers also deal with late rent payments and evictions, which can be difficult and require a solid understanding of the rental laws in a specific area. They also put a firm buffer between us and our tenants so that there aren't any personal feelings that can distract from the fact that our investment property is a business. Although we have sympathy for struggling tenants, we should not get involved in anything other than what we need to do to fulfill our lease obligations as a landlord. I've never met any of my tenants, just like I haven't met any of the people who work at the companies I invest in through purchasing corporate stocks. It's an investment and it's a business.

Let's talk a little about the factors that go into a real estate deal. We'll start with the ongoing costs of the property. We need to understand these figures before we get into a deal so that we can ensure we make a profit and have what's referred to as a free-cash-flow, income-producing asset. The primary expense for our rental will include our principal and interest (P&I) payment, any Homeowner's Association (HOA) payment(s), property insurance, annual taxes, the cost of hiring a property manager (if we outsource), and a cash reserve used for ongoing maintenance issues. The cash reserve can be larger or smaller depending on the age of the property and how much rehab has already been done. If we just put a new roof on, for example, then we don't have to worry about roof issues for another 15 or 20 years.

It's a good idea to have a couple of thousand set aside to handle ongoing issues like when the refrigerator needs repair. For larger projects (like putting in a new air conditioner), we'll need to save a portion of the rent over time and save the cash to pay for that expense. So we'll include a line item for the monthly cost that incorporates saving for large maintenance items—for example, we might save $20 or $30 per month for 5 years because we know the A/C will need replacing then. We then need to assess the market and get a sense of what we can rent the property out for once we've completed the rehab. The difference between the rent and the monthly cost is the passive cash flow we'll gain from the investment.

Once we've run all the monthly cost numbers and identified the rent, we have the cash flow. That's our profit. We can then reverse-engineer a purchase price that will allow the deal to make financial sense. The deal makes financial sense when we can purchase, rehab, refinance and rent on a positive cash flow basis. Put differently, the purchase price needs to be low enough for us to be able to spend money rehabbing the property and then refinance the property at an amount that is equal to or greater than the amount of money we'll have in the property through the purchase and rehab.

The purchase price and rehab costs will eventually be the P&I portion of the monthly expense because we'll be taking a mortgage out on the property once the rehab is completed and we have rented the unit. The mortgage is used to get our money back out of the deal so that we can get to our next real estate deal. Once we've gotten our money back out of the deal through the refinancing, we need to do the math on the difference between the rent and the monthly costs with the new refinanced mortgage. If the numbers are positive— meaning we make money each month—then we have an income-producing asset that didn't cost us anything because we got our money out of the deal after we refinanced. You can find out a lot of information online regarding this strategy if you simply search for "buy rehab refinance." There's a great book that you can read on this topic titled 'BRRRR' by David Mason. BRRRR stands for Buy, Rehab, Rent, Refinance, Repeat.

Let's spend a minute discussing the rehab. We'll want to match the rehab of the house to the local market/neighborhood. If we're in a high-end neighborhood, we need to lean towards nicer stainless-steel appliances and upgrades in places like the kitchen and bathroom(s). We can get a higher monthly rent if we do a higher-end rehab in such a neighborhood. If the neighborhood is mainstream, purchasing stainless-steel appliances won't demand any more rent and in fact will only detract from our profits. Don't feel like you need to make the rehab match your own home! Gauge the neighborhood by looking at other rental homes in the same area and replicate what you see. Renters can be hard on properties, so although things like vinyl plank flooring might cost more to install than carpet, it's a worthwhile investment because it lasts ten times longer and it's hard for renters to destroy. Look at the rehab as an investment that must have a sufficient return. At the same time, don't do things that are over and above the standard for the neighborhood, because you won't likely see an increase in rent for doing so.

I mentioned HOA costs which stands for Home Owners Association fees. The HOA fee is often times used to maintain shared spaces in a neighborhood, like neighborhood parks. HOA fees differ for each neighborhood. Some don't have any HOA. Some HOA fees include lawncare and maintenance on the exterior of the home (paint/roof), and some handle just the bare minimum. HOAs can be challenging—it's important to find one that has a good board, has sufficient cash reserves to handle forecasted maintenance, and isn't running a deficit. If the HOA is in debt or hasn't accrued cash for future expenses, then there is a high probability that a special assessment will be imposed on the homeowners. That's a one-time payment over and above the regular HOA fee that is used to fund projects that haven't been properly forecasted and accrued (saved up for).

Do your research on HOAs and make sure they're adequately funded! Also, assess what's included in the HOA fee. For example, if the HOA fee includes the exterior of the condo or townhouse you'll be purchasing, then you don't need to worry about saving for that expense. If certain costs are included in the HOA, you can deduct those ongoing maintenance costs when running the numbers for a potential real estate investment.

Now let's discuss the details behind a positive cash flow real estate investment. The math is quite easy once we've accounted for the various expenses. For example, let's say we have a $100,000 mortgage on the property after we've purchased it and completed the rehab. We're able to rent out the property for $1,200 per month. In this example, our monthly P&I might be around $500 (depending on our interest rate and mortgage period of 30 years or 15 years). Our monthly insurance cost might be around $120 and taxes might be $175 per month for homes in this price range. We've also decided to hire a property manager, which costs us 10% of the rent or $120 per month, and we want to save $25 per month for ongoing maintenance. The total monthly costs are $500 (P&I) + $120 (insurance) + $200 (taxes) + $120 (property manager) + $25 (saved for maintenance) = $965. Our profit each month is $235 ($1,200 rent minus $965 in costs). Over time, we will be able to raise the rent, so the income should slowly increase because our P&I will remain flat (assuming we took out a fixed mortgage).

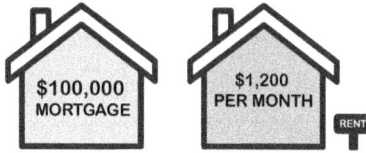

| $100,000 MORTGAGE | $1,200 PER MONTH | RENT |

| $500 + | $120 + | $200 + | $120 + | $25 = | $965 |
| MONTHLY P&I | MONTHLY INSURANCE COST | MONTHLY TAXES | PROPERTY MANAGER | MONTHLY MAINTENANCE | MONTHLY COSTS |

| $1,200 MONTHLY RENT | − | $965 MONTHLY COSTS | = | $235 PROFIT |

A great deal is a house that we can purchase, rehab, and then take out a mortgage that's equal to what we've invested (purchase price + rehab cost). That said, there will be instances where we have some cash tied up. In my example, let's say our purchase and rehab costs total $120,000 and we've taken out a $100,000 mortgage. We then have $20,000 tied up in the house. In the last example with the same expenses, we were making $235 per month or $2,820 per year. That means we're making a 14% return on our $20,000 ($2,820 / $20,000 = 14%). The stock market typically returns 7% to 8%. This comparison shows how investing in real estate can expedite our passive income strategy.

$120,000
PURCHASE AND REHAB

$100,000
MORTGAGE

= $20,000
TIED UP IN
THE HOUSE

$$\frac{\$2,820 \text{ YEARLY PROFIT}}{\$20,000 \text{ TIED UP IN THE HOUSE}} = 14\% \text{ RETURN ON } \$20,000$$

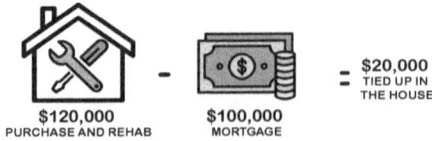

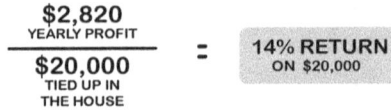

Buying and holding requires us to put risk mitigations in place in case something occurs at one of our properties. We should always require (in our lease) that our tenants have renter's insurance, and we also need to maintain our own insurance policy that has rental coverage for each property. It's also a good idea to open a Limited Liability Corporation (LLC) for our properties. The LLC removes us as individuals from any liability from a tenant. Some people suggest that we should have an LLC for each property, but I personally have one LLC for all of my properties and then have what's called an "umbrella policy," which is large enough to handle potential litigation risks. The umbrella policy covers unforeseen liabilities or problems with tenants. (For example, getting injured while in the home.) If the umbrella policy isn't large enough to cover potential litigation, then we run the risk of the policy not fully covering the cost of a lawsuit. Assets in the LLC can be seized to make up any shortfall between the judgment (say, from the accident on our property) and the policy amount. But we shouldn't get too hung on these points, although it's important that we understand how to limit our risk exposure and protect our assets. Setting up an LLC with an umbrella policy helps do just that. The LLC also helps keep expenses for the properties aligned, so our tax preparation becomes a little more organized. To be clear, the LLC has no tax benefit. The LLC is only used to mitigate the risks of us being personally exposed to litigation.

Buy and Flip

Those are the nuts and bolts of the buy-and-hold strategy. The other popular strategy is to purchase and flip properties. It's essentially the same, except that after purchasing and rehabbing, we sell the home. Some people just don't want to be a landlord, and that's okay. Buying and flipping can be a very lucrative side hustle if we make the right purchase up front.

Being handy is a helpful trait when deploying the buy-and-flip strategy because being able to do at least some of our own repairs obviously reduces the rehab cost. We can get tangible experience with rehabs by volunteering for programs like Habitat for Humanity. Many large home improvement stores also put on workshops that teach everything from hanging drywall to installing cabinets. Learn all you can so that you're able to take on smaller projects on your own!

Some people outsource all of the needed home repairs to a contractor. This can be a great option if the purchase price of the home is low enough to allow us to purchase it, incur rehab costs and then sell with enough profit to make the effort worthwhile. Many buy-and-flip investors see returns in the 20% to 30% range. We really just need to get smart regarding a specific market and know what newly remodeled homes are selling for in our real estate investment target ZIP code(s). That means looking for homes that are very dated and need to be refreshed and then doing the math on rehab costs and assessing the profit potential of each property.

We can use a few helpful data points to understand whether the home we're looking to purchase will be a good investment. For example, I typically look at the ratings of the schools, the population growth for the area, the job growth for the area, the rent-to-value ratio and the vacancy rates in the neighborhood. The rent-to-value (R:V) ratio is where we divide the monthly rent for the property by the purchase price. The higher the ratio of rent to value, the better the investment. An R:V ratio approaching or more than 1% is generally a good investment. Schools and neighborhood dynamics are important factors that drive demand for rental locations.

$$\underset{\text{RATIO}}{\text{R:V}} = 1\%$$

Tax Benefits of Real Estate Investing

Another important aspect of real estate investing is the tax benefits. As we've mentioned elsewhere in this book, the government generally encourages home ownership as well as investments in real estate. Real estate investors provide an important service to the market, and the government recognizes this fact.

First of all, income from real estate is taxed like normal income. So if we net an extra $25,000 per year in rents collected, that's simply added to our active income (just like the income from our 9-to-5 job) and taxed using the tax bracket in line with the US progressive tax system (we'll talk more about the US tax system later in the guide). However, real estate investing comes with a number of deductions. One is that real estate investing allows us to deduct all of the expenses from the rent that's collected. This means that all the monthly costs related to P&I, insurance, and taxes are deducted from our rental income. We're only taxed on the net income, which is the difference between the rent and all monthly costs. In my example earlier in this section, the net rent we received was $235 per month—that's the net income from the $1,200 rent minus all of the monthly expenses like HOA fees and property management fees. We can also deduct any repairs that occur throughout the year from our monthly net income.

All of this makes sense and is fair because then we're only taxed on our profits. The concept of depreciation, though, is the real key to real estate investing. Depreciation accounts for the fact that property has a determinable useful life, meaning that a home wears out over time and loses value if improvements aren't made. (The roof might not need to be replaced this year, but it will eventually.) Depreciation allows the real estate investor to separate the cost of the land from the building, and then the building value is divided by around 30 years (depending on the methodology). We can then deduct that amount from our net proceeds each year for the next 30 years.

Because the tax code is always evolving, we'll want to talk to an accountant about the specifics of depreciation and taxes. At this point, let's just talk about the concept of deprecation. We'll go back to our example of a property that has a $100,000 mortgage and nets $2,820 in passive income per year after all the expenses are deducted (the $235 per month example). Let's say that when we deduct the land value, we have a home value assessed at, say, $50,000. That makes the $100,000 value of the property 50% home and 50% land. When identifying depreciation, we divide the $50,000 home value (not the land value) by 30 years (the deprecation timeline) to get $1,666 in deprecation each year.

For tax purposes, the $2,820 in net income is then reduced by the depreciation of $1,666, resulting in the taxable income of $1,154 per year. We still have the $2,820 in our checking account, but the amount of taxes we owe has been reduced by the depreciation of the physical asset (the home), resulting in a reduced tax burden. Depreciation can be carried over to the next year if our income is lower than the depreciation amount. For example, if we had to install a new $2,000 air conditioner, then our net rental income would be reduced to $820 ($2,820 minus $2,000), but we would still have $1,666 in depreciation for the year. We can essentially eliminate all taxes due that year because we have $820 in rental income but we have $1,666 in depreciation.

DEPRECIATION DEDUCTION

$50,000
HOUSE

÷

30
YEARS
YEARS OF
DEPRECIATION

=

$1,666
DEPRECIATION
DEDUCTION PER YEAR

DEPRECIATION TAX BENEFIT

$2,820
YEARLY PROFIT

−

$1,666
ANNUAL
DEPRECIATION

=

$1,154
ACTUAL TAXED
AMOUNT

DEPRECIATION TAX BENEFIT WITH RENTAL EXPENSE

$2,820
YEARLY PROFIT

−

$1,666
ANNUAL
DEPRECIATION

−

$2,000
AIR CONDITIONING
EXPENSE

=

(-$846)
ACTUAL TAXED AMOUNT
CARRIED OVER TO NEXT YEAR
(NO TAXES DUE THIS YEAR)

NEXT YEAR'S TAX AMOUNT

$2,820
YEARLY PROFIT

−

$1,666
ANNUAL
DEPRECIATION

−

-$846
LAST YEAR'S
TAX CARRYOVER

=

$308
NEXT YEAR'S
TAX AMOUNT

That year, we'll deduct $1,666 in deprecation from the $820 in rental income, leaving a negative number of ($846). We'll have $846 ($1,666 in depreciation minus $820 in net rental income after the A/C cost) in taxes that can be carried over to next year's taxes. We can deduct $2,512 ($1,666 + $846 = $2,512) in depreciation next year so that our taxable income is only $308 for the next year ($2,820 in net rental income minus $1,666 in depreciation minus $846 in last year's carryover).

I'll add that making improvements to a home adds back to the assessed value of the home. In my example, the $50,000 home value was depreciated over 30 years, but if we put on a new roof that costs $5,000, then the asset value goes up to $55,000, and the annual depreciation value goes up for the remaining 30 years of the depreciation timeline. So we can continue to make improvements and investments in our property and increase the depreciation we can deduct each year after the additional investment is made.

Funding and Finding Properties

You might be thinking, "Okay, but how am I going to purchase an investment property?" Good question! Finding the initial capital to fund our first purchase can be challenging. The key is to look for creative ways to fund our purchases. Many people will simply use Step #6 to save up for their first purchase, which makes sense—if we've managed our credit score well, we can put down 20% and mortgage the property. We can then save our rental income and save our earnings from our 9-to-5 job to purchase our next property. If we save enough, we can purchase the next home and do the rehab with cash, then take out a mortgage to get our money back, as discussed earlier in this section. We get our money back and then do the same thing again and continue to build our rental portfolio. Again, finding a distressed property where the rehab makes a substantial change in the appraised value is essential.

I should point out that we won't likely find the right property right away. It's a good idea to work with either a realtor or a wholesaler so that they can keep an eye out for such properties. Another point is that we might find ourselves in need of additional cash during the rehab part of the process. There are options for this funding, one being "hard money lenders." The interest rates are very high for this kind of loan, so we need to make sure the rehab project has a realistic timeline, and we have to push hard *not* to have delays, because any delay in being able to refinance and rent out the property extends our loan and costs us a lot more money in interest. Or we can find partners who have money (capital) to lend but don't have the motivation to get into real estate. There are also owner-financed properties where the current owner will allow us to make payments to them over time so that no bank is needed for the purchase.

Another option is to go online. Plenty of social media groups discuss lending, and if we frequent those groups, there's a good chance we'll find investors who might be interested in the investment opportunities we've found. A simple search for "funding real estate investments" will provide plenty of guidance around funding our projects.

Owning real estate offers great diversification within our asset portfolio. Often times, people only have stocks in theirs. Stocks are great! For one thing, they don't consume our time if we purchase broad market index investments. But real estate provides a predictable income stream for many people, where the rents come in each month and then pay for life's expenses. Stocks and mutual funds have the benefit of liquidity (being able to convert quickly to cash), whereas real estate property is typically a longer-term investment unless we're in the flipping game. Another disadvantage of stocks is that they go up and down quickly and can lose value during times when we might need income.

If we're working on building up our assets and we have the goal of achieving financial independence, then we need to have a solid income stream to pay for our lifestyle...and if the stock market crashes, we won't want to sell our stock to pay for life-style expenses. In comparison, rental income often benefits from a stock downturn. That's because, unfortunately, market down-turns are often related to job losses, and when people lose their jobs, they're forced to sell their homes. Rental demand often increases during periods of stress for this reason. As the econ-omy improves, job availability increases, so people start buy-ing homes again. That creates vacancies in rentals, which are then often quickly swept up by individuals who want to move away from family or roommates now that they have a steady job. Rentals see activity and demand in most market conditions as long as we're making the necessary investments to keep our properties in good shape and desirable to renters.

Being a real estate investor doesn't have to be a complex or scary endeavor—it's simply about finding the right property that will be cash-flow-producing after we've done all the nec-essary rehab. Time and patience are key. After having read this chapter, hopefully now you have some ideas about real estate investing and might want to look into more resources on the subject. Numerous groups of people (online and through investing clubs) are open to helping newbies. Just get smarter about the subject through self-learning and be open to opportunities!

111

LIFE PRO TIP *Landlords sometimes get a bad rap for being greedy. This is true in some cases, but most of the time, the increase in rent is being used to pay for increases in taxes and insurance that the landlord must pay. We will likely be renters ourselves early in life, so it's good to understand why rents go up. Landlords raise rents over time because their own costs go up. The increase in rent does not go directly into the landlord's pockets—their costs increase each year. The landlord also needs to make a return on their investment, as is the case with any business. I bring this up so that you can have a perspective from both sides – the tenant and the landlord.*

The Stock Market

This is another heavy topic that earns the AP assignation. While this subject might not be of great interest to some people, understanding the broad concepts related to stocks will bring lifetime benefits!

Buying stocks (sometimes called "equities") can be confusing, but it's a vital part of building wealth and being financially secure. Investing in stocks is how most people create household wealth outside of their homes (assuming they own and don't rent). Unlike real estate—which entails a long exit process—stocks are very liquid (can easily be sold) and allow owners to sell on almost a real-time basis. While we're going to be focusing on how to understand individual stocks, know that the "easiest" way to participate in the stock market is to purchase broad low-cost mutual funds like the total market funds by Fidelity (FSKAX) and Vanguard

(VTSAX). Both of these allow us to have exposure to a wide and diversified set of US companies.

My intention in this section is not to arm us with all of the details required to comprehensively assess a company's stock. Rather, let's understand the broad variables we should look at if we're thinking about purchasing the stock of an individual company, like Apple or General Electric. Throughout our lives, people will tell us about individual stocks and give us tips on which stocks they believe will go up over time. Many people will take that advice and make an investment…but because they don't understand why that particular stock might be "good" or "bad," they're really just gambling on someone else's recommendation. We need to have a broad understanding of stocks in order to do a little digging into specific recommendations.

Market Capitalization, Stock Splits and Reverse Splits

Many people think they're getting a good deal if a stock price is low—the actual price for the individual stock isn't high, so it must be a good deal, right? The stock price makes it look cheap. Conversely, people are apprehensive about purchasing a stock that costs a couple hundred or a couple thousand dollars. But in reality, the individual stock price tells us nothing about how expensive the stock actually is.

Every company has what's referred to as **market capitalization.** That's the company's worth as determined by the stock market. We can go to any financial website and see any company's market cap. The price of a stock is just the market cap divided by the number of outstanding shares. So if a company's market cap is $100 and there are 10 outstanding shares, then the price per share will be $10 ($10 per share x 10 shares = $100 market cap). The same company has the right to increase the number of shares by splitting each share in half (a

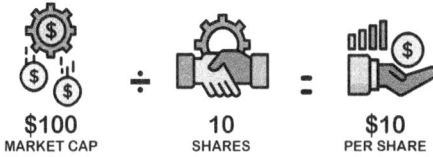

$100
MARKET CAP

10
SHARES

$10
PER SHARE

stock split), or they can go the other direction and reduce the number of outstanding shares by doing what's called a **reverse split**. Don't be confused by these terms—a stock split is just doubling the number of outstanding shares, which reduces the price of each share by half.

To be clear, the market cap doesn't change if the company splits its shares. It just means that while the market cap of $100 stays the same, if there's a stock split in our example, there are now 20 shares, not 10. The same market cap is then divided by 20 shares, resulting in a new stock price of $5 per share. If we owned one share of the $10 stock before the split, then we'd have two shares after the split, each valued at $5. We still own $10 of the company.

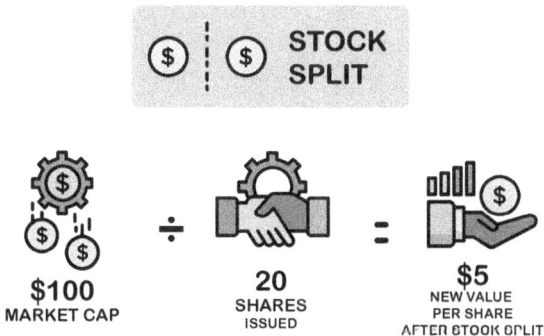

$** | **$ **STOCK SPLIT**

$100
MARKET CAP

20
SHARES
ISSUED

$5
NEW VALUE
PER SHARE
AFTER STOCK SPLIT

A reverse split is the opposite—a company can reduce the number of shares by reverse splitting. Again, using our example, then the company would only have 5 shares, where each share is worth $20. The market cap of $100 is the same, but the stock price has doubled. Many people will then think it's expensive, but the market cap hasn't changed, and the market cap is how much the company is valued by the market.

Companies typically split their stock so that retail investors can more easily purchase their shares. If the company's sales grow quickly, then the market cap will also go up. That's because the market monitors quarterly earnings from the company and thus values the company more because its sales are going up. When sales go up, the chances of investors getting a higher return on their investment also go up. That increased revenue will (or should) eventually be paid back to the shareholders—that's the people who own shares in the company—through dividends. The market cap will likely climb, and if the number of shares remains the same (meaning the company doesn't split the stocks), then the price per share goes up along with the market cap.

Retail investors might not want to purchase shares that cost hundreds or thousands of dollars, so over time, the company will conduct stock splits to make the individual share prices lower. But that just means there are now twice as many shares outstanding after the split. If we already owned shares, then we have twice as many shares after the split, and we still hold the same total value of shares. The split just makes the stock price lower so that retail investors who have $50 to invest can buy a share. Prior to the split—when the share price was $100—those same investors would not have bought a share.

So companies split their shares to encourage more trades because they know that retail investors are more likely to purchase lower-priced shares. But the stock split didn't actually change the market cap, which is the real value of the company. Some companies don't ever split their shares because they don't want high volatility in their share prices (which often comes along with low-priced shares). People might enter and exit shares that cost $20, but they might not trade a stock that's valued at, say, $2,500 as often. Some stocks are priced at well over $100,000 per share because they've never been split. (See Berkshire Hathaway's stock, which was trading for over $400,000 per share at the time this book was written – Berkshire Hathaway is the company Warren Buffett runs.) Average retail investors aren't buying and selling $100,000 stocks because of the capital involved, so the stock price is more steady over time.

But here's the thing—in reality, the $100,000 stock might be a lot cheaper than the $20 stock because the overall market cap of the $100,000 stock is lower than what the company is actually worth. The $20 stock might be less money to buy but might be way more expensive (or overvalued) because the market cap is overvalued by the market, meaning that it's too high when its future forecasted sales are compared to the future forecasted sales of its peers.

We can have two identical companies with the same market cap, but if one has twice as many shares being traded, then the other one will appear "cheaper" because the stock is half the price. However, because the market cap is the same, the value of the individual stock is the same despite the fact that one cost twice as much as the other. Many people purchase so-called "penny stocks" because they think they're cheap, but splitting shares to make them *appear* cheap is a trick that many retail investors fall for. Don't invest in a stock because the share price is low or high—invest because you understand the company and think it's going to grow over time.

The P/E Ratio

In short, the market cap reflects the real value of the company. Another way to measure whether a stock is undervalued is by studying the company's P/E ratio, or price-to-earnings ratio. The **P/E ratio** provides the multiple (ratio) that investors are willing to pay for each dollar of profit (earnings) per share. If a company has a higher P/E ratio than what its peers have, then the company is either forecasted to grow more quickly than its peers, or the company might be overvalued.

Let's break this down into basic terms. The P/E ratio = price per share / earnings per share. Let's say a company is trading at $20 per share. The company might have a total of 100,000 shares outstanding and have a total earnings (net income) of $75,000 for the year. Total earnings is just the total amount of net income that a company makes. Its net income is the total revenue (sales) minus the company's costs, like what it pays for salaries and rent.

In my example, the company's earnings is $75,000. Divide that by the number of shares (100,000), and that's $0.75 per share. Therefore, the company makes a profit of $0.75 per share that's outstanding. The P/E ratio is $20 (the share price) / $0.75 (earnings per share) = 26.67. That means investors are willing to pay $26.67 for every dollar of net income the company produces. The same company can have twice as many shares outstanding, say 200,000 shares. But the price per share is half that amount, so it's now $10 because there are twice as many shares. However, the P/E ratio is the same. We have the same $75,000 in net income, but we now have 200,000 shares, so the earnings per share is $75,000 / 200,000 = $0.375. The P/E ratio is then $10 per share / $0.375 per share, making it the same 26.67.

EXAMPLE ONE: 100,000 SHARES

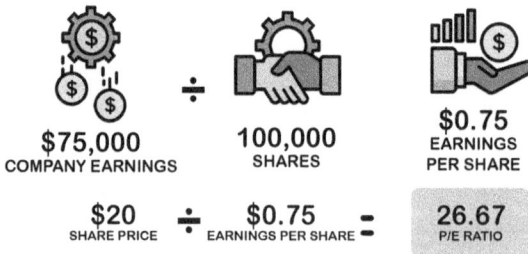

$75,000	100,000	$0.75
COMPANY EARNINGS	SHARES	EARNINGS PER SHARE

$20	$0.75	26.67
SHARE PRICE	EARNINGS PER SHARE	P/E RATIO

The reason the P/E ratio is important is that it is another good indicator as to whether a stock price is indeed cheap or expensive. If we look at two companies in the same industry that produce very similar goods and services and one P/E ratio is lower than the other, we can conclude that the one with the lower P/E ratio might be undervalued (meaning it's a better buy) because each share we buy represents more actual revenue per share when comparing the two. Let's go back to the beginning of this section and think about the friend who gave us a stock tip. If we do a little research, we can see what the P/E ratio is. If it has a very high multiple, then it's likely not an inexpensive stock because we aren't seeing much net income for each share. The higher the P/E ratio is, the more we're paying for every dollar of net income. The lower the P/E ratio is, the less we're paying for every dollar of net income.

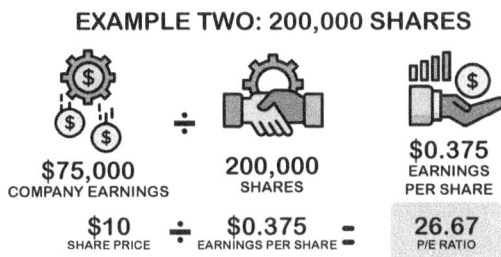

EXAMPLE TWO: 200,000 SHARES

$75,000 ÷ 200,000 = $0.375
COMPANY EARNINGS   SHARES   EARNINGS PER SHARE

$10 ÷ $0.375 = 26.67
SHARE PRICE   EARNINGS PER SHARE   P/E RATIO

Slow-Growing vs. Fast-Growing Industries

To put it in context, stocks that are in fast-growing industries will typically have P/E ratios of 30 or 40 or even over 100. This means the market is anticipating significant growth in that stock; in turn, that means investors think sales will rapidly increase in the future and are willing to pay a higher P/E multiple. Because they think the net income will be much higher in the future than it is now, they invest in the stock because they think the stock price will go up. Investors are willing to pay a higher P/E multiple because they believe the future earnings will go up.

The opposite is true for companies in slow-growing sectors (at the time of writing, the energy sector was one of these). Companies in slow-growing sectors have lower P/E ratios because their earnings are not expected to grow quickly, and therefore, today's investors won't pay a high P/E ratio because they don't expect the earnings per share to quickly increase.

But let's say that a company in a slow-growing sector suddenly has a new innovation. They announce it. Just as suddenly, the company has increased earnings in the future compared to what the market had originally expected. Once the new innovation is announced, the stock price sees a jump in the price per share. Investors are now willing to pay a higher multiple (or P/E ratio) because the future forecasted earnings went up, and therefore, the future earnings per share should go up. If that happens, then the share price will also go up because investors think that the future earnings per share will be higher, thus justifying a higher P/E ratio compared to the other companies that don't have access to the new innovative technology.

As a point of reference, the overall S&P P/E ratio has historically been in the 15 to 20 range. That's because although some tech companies might have a ratio of 80 or 90, companies in slow-growing industries have P/E ratios of maybe 9 or 10 or 11. That makes the blended S&P ratio around 15 to 20.

You might be wondering why investors would purchase stocks with low P/E ratios in slow-growing industries. These slow-growing companies are often mature, meaning they've been in business for a long time. With maturity comes a predictable income stream. The mature company isn't typically turning around and using its net income to make investments in innovation to grow

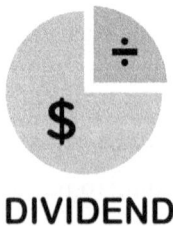

$10,000 **X** 3%
STOCK VALUE   DIVIDEND

$300
PER YEAR IN
DIVIDENDS

DIVIDEND

the business. Rather than making investments with their profits, the mature company will pay what's referred to as a dividend. A **dividend** is simply an amount per share that a company pays in cash to each shareholder. Most companies pay a dividend each quarter. A dividend-paying stock typically makes payments in the 1% to 5% range, meaning that the company will pay 1% to 5% dividend per share. If we owned $10,000 of stock, then we'd get $100 to $500 per year in dividends.

Fast-growing companies don't typically pay dividends because they think their profits are better spent on investments in their business, like building more manufacturing facilities to plan for future growth or investing in research and development (R&D) to be able to roll out the next generation of technology for their product. Investors who purchase individual stocks often have a combination of dividends stocks in slow-growing industries *and* growth stocks in fast-growing companies. The latter are purchased because the investor believes that the company is making the right investments in technology and that sales (and profits) will increase so that the stock price will also increase.

A good example of a dividend stock is an energy company like Duke Energy. It isn't growing fast, but it has a predictable revenue base from households paying their electric bill each month. The stock has a good dividend because it's not reinvesting huge sums of its profits into new products—instead, they're using the net proceeds to pay dividends to investors. The share price isn't likely to go up and down in big swings because their earnings are predictable, and investors like their predictable dividends. The older we get, the more we want dividend stocks. Why? They're less likely to lose value during market turmoil, and older investors want predictable dividends to pay their own bills. The prices of growth stocks go up and down quickly and are not great for investors who don't have a high risk tolerance for being able to stomach substantial changes in the values of their assets.

This section on stocks isn't intended to educate you on every aspect of how stocks are traded. (There are endless resources you can take advantage of if you want to be an expert.) The intention here is to arm you with the very basics of how you can quickly evaluate a company's stock and see if it's actually undervalued (again, meaning the company's P/E ratio is low compared to its peers). Doing this research will enable you to avoid the mistake of thinking that a stock is cheap just because it's a low-priced stock. Many low-priced stocks don't have any net income—the company actually loses money every year—and so they might not have any P/E ratio at all because there are no earnings. Making stock investments without any idea of the companies' underlying financial performance is a pure gamble. Unless you know something about a stock and are confident that the earnings of the company will go up for one reason or another, you should do your research before purchasing that stock.

Mergers and Acquisitions

I'll also add that companies with low P/E ratios are often targets for acquisition by other companies because the acquiring company feels that the low-ratio company's future sales aren't accurately forecasted. Or (and more importantly) the acquiring company thinks it would be a smart move to buy the other company and integrate that company's products into their own catalog—that way, it can reduce the associated costs of its product/service line by incorporating the products and knowledge of the acquired company into its existing portfolio.

If we have two individual companies making very similar products, that's two CEOs, two CFOs, two (or more) manufacturing plants and two sets of marketing, legal, etc., teams. Each company has its own set of expenses. One company can acquire the other and manufacture the product by making adjustments to its existing manufacturing process, plus it can reduce jobs by having only one CEO and one CFO and one operations team and one marketing team. Basically, all the expenses that come along with running a company can be evaluated, and many can be eliminated when one company is acquired and integrated into the acquiring company.

The net income of the acquiring company should go up

because they are now selling the acquired company's products at less cost because they got rid of duplicate job roles and duplicate manufacturing facilities. This should result in higher earnings per share for the acquiring company, prompting the stock price to go up for the acquiring company. The acquiring company might issue debt to buy out the shareholders of the acquired company and pay off the debt with earnings after the acquisition. This activity of one company acquiring another for the purposes of having a single company with higher earnings per share (versus the earnings per share if the two companies were still being run separately) is the basis of most merger and acquisition (M&A) activity. This is generally what is meant by the term "investment banking."

Initial Public Offering (IPO)

We might read about a hot initial public offering (IPO). An IPO happens when a private company goes to the market for the first time and issues shares that can be purchased by the public. The private company might be owned by individuals or by private equity investors. Private equity firms are investment

START-UP VALUED AT $100 MILLION

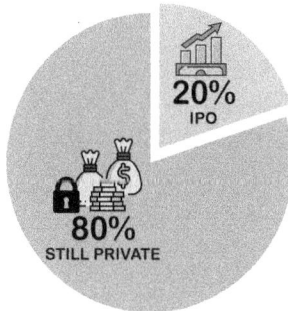

20%
IPO

80%
STILL PRIVATE

companies that use their money to make investments in start-ups; investors give these firms their money to invest on their behalf. Investing in private equity often requires that you meet certain net worth thresholds that evaluate whether or not you're a so-called "accredited investor." These safeguards are in place to keep retail investors from losing money, as private equity investing is quite risky.

The owners of a private equity company will have a "valuation" placed on the private company, and then shares are issued to reflect the valuation. Let's say a start-up company has a valuation of $100 million. The company might be owned by two private equity companies, each owning 50% of the stock in the company. The owners will decide how much money they want to raise through the IPO and then issue that amount of stock. For example, a private company wants to raise $20 million by going public. Two private equity companies could issue 1 million shares through an IPO where each share is priced at $20 per share. These two companies now own 80% of the equity, and 20% is being freely traded. The market cap of the company represents the overall value of the company, including all the shares being publicly traded plus the equity (shares) still owned by the private equity owners (i.e., their remaining 80%). In contrast, some IPOs sell all the shares upfront so that none of the private owners own anything after the IPO. Each IPO is different, but just understand that an IPO is the first time a private company's stock is available for the public to own.

Mindset for Success

Our definition of what "success" is will be unique to each of us, but there is one common thread shared by everyone who reaches their goals: having a mindset that facilitates success. Having the right mindset and framework for success is just as important as developing goals and taking action. If we don't believe in ourselves and our ability to reach our goals, then we'll be working against our innate ability to be successful.

Sometimes we tell ourselves that we can't have something or we can't do something. We have to start our journey to success by acknowledging that anything is possible for us if we develop a plan and then actually act on the first step of the plan. In order to see progress and continued positive momentum toward our goals, we have to believe those goals are possible. We need to truly believe that it's just a matter of time until we get there. We cannot let limitations in our minds dictate our future. We can't let our backgrounds and past life experiences limit us. We have to have a positive attitude, and we can't stop if we run into problems or failures—instead, we need to embrace them and view them as challenges in life that we need to overcome.

Challenges and problems are a big part of everyone's life. It's how we react to those problems that make a difference. We can't give up on ourselves or our goals and dreams when we face inevitable failures and setbacks. What we're doing today won't yield benefits until maybe a year or even 5 or 10 years down the road, but the benefits will come if we push past the hurdles along the way. Yes, failure will happen, but if we get up and try something different and keep trying, we will eventually succeed. We have to look at failure as a lesson learned and then learn from the failure. That's how we learn what *not* to do.

It's not going to be easy! You will doubt yourself and think it isn't possible to achieve your goal, but it is! Just keep going and trying, and you will get there.

SELF-TALK AND OUR
PERCEPTION OF OURSELVES

We all have an internal voice that interprets our environment and allows us to assess situations, other people, and ourselves. We have conversations in our heads with that voice. It's important, though, to control what we think about. Even though we know it's not healthy, many of us let our minds wander into unproductive territory. We think about the highlights in our life, but we also run reels of not-so-great moments that we regret.

Because our internal self-talk is ongoing, it's important to recognize when it isn't being helpful and might actually be holding us back. Many of our internal voices are destructive and may limit us. Negative self-talk focuses on our shortcomings—it's the voice that tells us we don't have the education or experience to pursue the next promotion at work. It's the voice that lets us be intimidated by others or think we're not able to compete at a higher level. It's the voice that makes us unsure of ourselves to the point where maybe we don't pursue a business interest. It makes us doubt what we see and think when we look in the mirror.

All of this is extremely important to assess—we need to consciously understand what we're telling ourselves. Many of us catch ourselves in negative talk. We might be constantly stressed about a situation in the future that likely won't occur; we might constantly play out the worst-case scenario over and over. Make it a point to stop yourself when you recognize this happening. Stop and think about whether you can actually solve the future problem you're worried about. If it's something you can't control, then don't worry about it because worrying won't solve anything. It's of course easier to say than do, but you should really only concern yourself with scenarios you can control and take action on. Be optimistic about how things will come together in the future.

You control the way you think about yourself, and what you think of yourself should be uplifting and encouraging. *You* control your self-image. If you're not happy with it, then acknowledge that and do something about it. Don't live a life where you're unhappy with yourself for one reason or another. You can take the necessary (and often hard) steps you need to take to become more confident! If taking a course on a specific topic might improve your chances of a promotion, then do that. If going to the gym is necessary for you to be confident about the way you look, then do that. And use the confidence you're building to improve your self-talk.

Our self-talk needs to be positive and optimistic. While that's common knowledge, it isn't commonly practiced. We should acknowledge that it's natural to try to find potential issues or obstacles that keep us from reaching for our goals. Our negative self-talk often tells us it's too hard to do something, and then we don't try—we might think, "I don't have time for that" or "I can't do that because of [insert excuse]." It might be hard or uncomfortable to take the next step, so our brain gives us an out and provides us with reasons why we can't do something.

Catch yourself when your self-talk tells you that you can't do something! You can train your brain to think about how you can accomplish the next step. The key is to catch negative self-talk and reshape the situation to think about the next step. And then do it! Don't think about how hard it will be or how long it will take—just focus on the very next step and do that. Take one step at a time.

OUR PAST SELF – MISTAKES, EMBARRASSING MOMENTS, AND FAILURES

Our self-talk can be very hard on us when we make mistakes. We tend to dwell on our mistakes and failures and use them as excuses not to pursue a goal. We stop trying because we've failed the last five times and we don't have the energy to try again. We stop. We get off track and we quit. We tell ourselves we can't do anything else to get back on track to success, that there's just no way to get out of a hole or that a goal just isn't possible because of [insert excuse].

We might relive embarrassing moments, too, but dwelling on the negatives of a situation only brings us down—it has absolutely no benefit. We'll handle that situation differently the next time because we learned from our past. We can adjust and try a different approach the next time. Maybe we can't interview well, so we don't pursue advancements at work, or we think we're missing some skill and therefore don't actively pursue a promotion. We can take the necessary steps to bridge the gap in why we think we can't achieve a specific goal.

Each one of us controls our future, and only *you* can take the necessary steps that will allow you to achieve your goals. Consider what you learned from the situation. How have you grown since then? Reflecting on a situation and wishing you had handled it differently shows you've developed since then. You're a different person over time because of your experiences. You've grown from that situation, so you shouldn't wish it hadn't happened or beat yourself up that it did. That experience was necessary to allow you to reach where you are right now.

Learning from and acting upon our own mistakes is important. We should also recognize that when we see others fail or make mistakes, that often shapes what we think is possible for ourselves. Maybe our friend purchased an investment property and regretted her investment. She bought during a market peak, so she took a big loss when the market crashed in 2008.

You remember that situation and have taken real estate investing off the table. But don't use that example as an excuse not to do your own research and find out why that kind of investing didn't work for your friend! Learn from the failures of others, and don't be fearful of a situation because someone else failed. That mistake shouldn't be a reason to tell ourselves we'll also fail. If your goal is to own property, then think about the immediate next step. Maybe that's buying a book about real estate investments. Start to learn about the subject; build up your knowledge and therefore your confidence. Don't internalize stories of failures of others and limit what you think is possible for you.

Sometimes failure is debilitating. It can be a downward spiral if we let it. But deep inside of us, we have a personal drive that needs to be turned on. All of us have that drive, but it is often covered with past failures and regret and shame from actions taken years ago. Acknowledge the pain and the failures and the moments of embarrassment and let them go.

People who constantly bring up past failures or embarrassing moments aren't people we need in our life. They are toxic people, and they will limit us. These people are not positive influences and will only inhibit us from reaching our goals. People who *are* in our corner will encourage us to move on and acknowledge the past but not let it impede our future. We won't forget the lessons we learned from our past actions! We'll carry those lessons with us forever so that we won't make the same mistake twice.

That said, we don't have to continually relive the past in order to learn from it. It's critical to recognize when we're doing this and stop by telling ourselves that what happened is in the past and that our future is not shaped by our past mistakes. It's shaped by who we are *now*, and we've grown as a result of those past mistakes. We're different and better people as a result of our past.

WE CONTROL OUR OWN FUTURE

The foundational work we're doing now to achieve our goals will benefit one person: our future self. That said, while it's easy to fantasize about our future self, often times, we're so focused on the future that we forget life is happening right now. We must learn to enjoy the journey and recognize that the process is what leads to success. Success definitely won't come easy, and we'll have a lot of setbacks, but that's expected. We need to think about how the decisions we make today will affect our life in 10 years. If we develop a plan and accept our failures and get back up and find the next opportunity, then we will one day look back and thank our past self. I'm always thinking back 10, 15, or even 20 years, and I'm grateful for the tough decisions that were made. Eventually, you will feel the same way.

Are you doing the tough things right now that your future self will benefit from? Failure is a part of the process—it's the only way we learn. It shows that we're trying, that we're actually taking action. *Not* failing is what we should really be worried about. We should also stay away from anyone who enjoys seeing us fail. Someone more successful than us will never find joy in our failure, nor will they discourage us. Why? Because they failed, too, and they kept going. They know that we can also accomplish what we want if we maintain a positive outlook and keep trying.

Aside from embracing failure, the other critical mindset to have is to know that we are in control of our lives. Yes, we might be given setbacks, and we might not have been born with the same advantages as others, but we can't control those variables. If we tell ourselves that we can't do something because of those setbacks, then we're simply falling into the trap of being a victim. Victims don't control their destiny—instead, they put up mental roadblocks as to why they can't find success. Those roadblocks allow them to quit or blame others or just accept what they have in life. Be a person who acknowledges life's disadvantages but who also accepts them and moves on.

People with a victim mindset fall behind on their dreams as each day and year goes by. In contrast, people with a creator mindset believe in themselves and their ability to shape their future. A creator mindset is empowering and allows us to believe that anything is possible, that we can be successful and that even though we've lost count of how many times we've failed, we still have the ability to pursue our dreams. We can acknowledge lessons learned and have an attitude that allows us to believe in a brand-new identity. We can create our new selves right now! We can shed what we believed to be our reality.

Being positive and finding the bright side of situations is a critical feature of having a creator mindset. We can't let negative thoughts fill our minds! We can't let any negative energy fill the space that should be used to reach our goals—we need that space to think of ways to accomplish what we want. There's always a way, but we likely won't find it if we're focusing on our past and allowing our past to dictate our future.

Our brain is hard to train, but we can do it. We can catch ourselves when we start to talk negatively to ourselves. As soon as we realize we're doing that, we can stop and tell ourselves that we're not the sum of our mistakes. We can start a new life right now and think about paths that will lead us to success. Focusing on positive self-talk is critical to having a positive and fulfilling life because *we will ultimately become what we believe we will be.* How we envision ourselves in our minds and how we envision good things coming into our lives is what will play out in our reality. This is sometimes referred to as the **law of attraction**.

Notice that I'm not positioning this as a theory or belief. That's because successful people don't question this force—we truly *can* control our future by focusing on the good things that will come into our lives. The same goes for having a victim mindset. If we focus our day on our past failures or how we'll never have a meaningful relationship or never have money, then that's what will continue to happen. We'll attract those outcomes, and we'll continue to see the things we don't actually want in our life.

Countless millionaires and billionaires agree that the power of positive thinking (and the law of attraction) has played a critical role in their life. Why wouldn't we give ourselves that benefit, too, and adjust our minds to focus on what we want in our lives and who we want to be? Positive thinking certainly can't hurt our chances of success! Believing that love or meaningful relationships or money will flow into their lives is a key attribute of successful people.

But that doesn't mean that we can just start *thinking* about living a meaningful life with wealth and success and it's going to happen. We have to develop our plan and take action. Still, our outcomes will be different if we have a mindset that envisions success and if we know we'll accomplish our goals. That might not happen next week or next month or next year, but it will happen if we continue to pursue the very next step that's needed to move toward our goals. And envision your life as though it's already happened. Focus mentally on what you want in your life, and don't think about the bad things that you don't. If we have a creator mindset and believe we will succeed, then we'll have the energy to accept failure for what it is—just another action we took that didn't work. We've learned that lesson and won't do it again. A creator mindset allows us to continue to focus on what we know will happen in our lives, and it will give us the motivation to think about other solutions we can try to pursue to accomplish our goals. A can-do attitude will eventually end in success if we're trying new things and we pick ourselves up to try something different.

In order to have control of our future, we have to acknowledge that our present self is a result of our past actions. If we don't believe that, then we can't believe we can change our life and make it what we want it to be. We're mentally limiting ourselves because we're allowing our minds to make excuses for not achieving our goals. What we do today and tomorrow and the next day and the next day *will be* who we are 5 years from now. This doesn't mean that we won't face outside influences, forces, and challenges, but it's how we react to those obstacles that shape the Future Us.

Our parents are not us; our childhood is not us. Our present self has been shaped by those experiences, but we have the power to change if we want to. We have the ability to shed all that baggage and create the person we want to be. Despite that, most of us are held back by what we perceive as limits. Most of us aren't even aware of these subconscious limitations, but they're firmly in place, and we need to question why. We need to identify our mental limitations and ask ourselves why we're not taking action on our goals.

Our biggest hurdles in life will be our self-image and our self-confidence in our abilities. We tell ourselves that we can't have financial success, or we can't go to college, or we can't work a part-time job to earn extra income because we think it's not possible for us, but why *can't* those things be our reality? Yes, we'll make mistakes along the way, but we'll learn and grow and the reward will be that much more enjoyable because of the challenging journey we undertook.

We need to tell ourselves that the next year or two are going to be hard but necessary, and we need to start our journey now and not give up. We need to enjoy the journey and the process because the journey *is* life. Life is long when looking through the windshield, but it's very short when looking through the rearview mirror—while the seconds are long, the years are short. We can't let time pass by while we're holding tight for a lucky break. There are exceptions like lottery winners, but the vast majority of people who are successful in life actually *aren't* lucky. They succeed because they have a hard work ethic and aren't afraid to fail, and when they do fail, they embrace the lesson. Maybe most importantly, they have confidence in themselves. They have moments of doubt, sure, but they pick themselves up and move on.

Successful people take inventory of their lives and focus on the things they can control. Then they take action toward their goals. There's no value in worrying about things we can't control

in life or dwelling on the past. Thinking about the past often results in regret, and thinking about the future typically results in
worrying. Doing either means we're stealing from the present,
and the present is our life! So let's not sell ourselves short and
believe the limitations in our minds. There's absolutely nothing
productive about believing that we can't do something or that
our past in some way will dictate our future.

> **LIFE PRO TIP** *Many successful people fully understand and
> subscribe to the notion that what you think about will eventually
> show up in your life. The Law of Attraction. We can take that
> one step further and develop a vision board to outline our goals.
> This board has images of the things we want to attract in our
> life, which helps reinforce our thoughts because it's a visual re-
> minder of what we expect will eventually be our reality. Search
> online for "vision board" and create your own if you want to
> take this philosophy to the next level.*

CONTINUALLY REINFORCING
THE NARRATIVE

In order to maintain our newfound positive mindset, we're going
to have to continually reinforce it and feed our minds with en-
couragement. We can't just read these passages and expect our
minds to be permanently changed, just like we can't work out
our biceps and expect to have results after an hour. We have to
continually work at having a positive mindset and consistently
feed our minds with positive reinforcement in order to break
the mindset that we currently have. If we don't train our mind
to focus on things we actually *can* control, then we'll fall back
into being too frightened to take action, and we'll keep focusing on our limitations instead of focusing on the steps we need
to take to meet our goals.

So many great books and videos reinforce positive thinking! Simply search for "positive thinking books" or view "motivational videos" on YouTube. Put on your headphones and listen to motivational messages every day for at least 20 or 30 minutes, preferably in the morning. Catch yourself when you start to recognize your mind shifting back to its old negative and defeatist ways. Train your brain to think the way you want it to think!

We've been conditioned to believe in our limitations and worry about outcomes, and unfortunately, that discourages us from taking calculated chances. Perhaps in the distant past, that was a good framework, back when prehistoric humans were defending themselves from risks we don't really face today. Those behavioral survival instincts probably saved us from danger and kept us alive. But again, even though many of those risks no longer exist, we still fear taking chances.

FAILING TO TAKE ACTION

Let's talk a little about why we don't take action to reach our goals. Often times, it comes down to feeling anxious or nervous about a potential outcome. It's easier to ignore or delay taking action and just keep doing what we're doing. In our minds, the inertia of getting started is too hard to overcome, so we put off doing something until later...and then we put it off again. We might think about it next week, but then our nerves and anxiety kick in, and once again, we ignore what we know is the right next step for us.

When we step back and think about why we have anxiety about taking action, it's almost always because we don't have the experience or knowledge of how to do that task. Public speaking is commonly recognized as being something that people fear doing, but if we were asked to get on a stage and discuss a topic or hobby we know very well, and we did this on numerous occasions, we'd eventually get up there and naturally deliver our comments because we know the content and we've done it before. Likewise, if we're nervous about getting our finances in order, it's probably because we fear what we might find. But once we tackle that fear and do the work to understand the issues, then we'll find that we're not nervous anymore because we understand the details and know the possible outcomes. We're knowledgeable about the subject and are no longer concerned about the unknown because we now have a known plan. We know how to identify and handle potential outcomes. And we typically don't fear what we know.

This holds true for just about everything in life. If we've done our research or already experienced something, we're not going to be nearly as nervous or hesitant about it. This is why taking action is so important—we'll always be nervous about taking the necessary steps to achieve success if we don't have any experience under our belt. We'll be more confident once we actually start a business or purchase our first real estate investment or apply for higher education. Doing something that's scary and (often) failing is a prerequisite for success. It's what breaks through the inertia that we all experience. *Not* doing things that are hard or scary is what holds us back from becoming who we can eventually become.

One more point on being nervous and anxious: I like to think of these feelings as being the necessary energy that's required to get us motivated and in the right mindset. Being nervous is nothing more than energy. It's not weakness, which is how many people interpret those feelings. No, it's simply our body gearing up for an important event. I've found that this view on nerves has helped me become more calm and collected when I'm feeling nervous and anxious.

Yet another reason many people don't take action is that they doubt their own intelligence and overestimate the intelligence of others. This is related to what's called "imposter syndrome," which happens when we feel we're not really deserving of an accomplishment because we think we lack the intelligence or experience to be where we're at in life. But the truth is, we don't have to be considered "smart" to be successful. The common thread with successful people isn't their intelligence but rather their work ethic and their ability to look for opportunities by being positive and not being afraid to fail. While some people naturally learn through book reading and can quickly retain new information, those aren't skills required to succeed. And while intelligence might provide a bit of an edge, it's not the deciding factor when it comes to whether or not people will live successful lives. Perseverance is much more valuable, and anyone can persevere if they make the decision to do so.

What are you doing this afternoon or tomorrow to improve life for your future self? What are the little improvements you're going to make that will add up over time so that in 10 years, you're in a different place? Are you going to start looking for a more challenging job with better pay, and if so, what skills do you need to realistically get hired? Are you going to set up a budget to live within your means, giving yourself the chance to start to execute the 7 steps? Maybe you're going to try to find a distressed investment property that you can possibly rehab to add to your personal balance sheet, or maybe you're going to look into going back to school.

Decide on your future goals and start doing the little things that add up to big change. Starting is the hardest part! Don't get bogged down by how long the journey is going to be. Focus on the initial steps that will get you on the path to meeting your goals. You will have setbacks, yes, but persevering through those challenges is how you will achieve greatness and live the lifestyle you choose. Life is passing by, and before you know it, it will be 10 years down the road. It really is true that the minutes pass slowly but the years go quickly. You'll increasingly agree with this as you get older. I know I do—I can't believe how quickly the last 15 years have gone by!

Decide right now that you're going to live the lifestyle you want and put a plan in place that gets you there. We are responsible for our own life and outcomes, and nobody's coming to rescue us—we must take control of our situation and demand more both *of* and *for* ourselves. Waiting around to pursue our goals only gives us less time to enjoy the benefits once we've accomplished what we set out to do. It's like people remodeling their homes right before they put them on the market. They could have enjoyed those new floors and remodeled bathrooms if they had done the work earlier in life rather than getting around to it "later." Later will be here before you know it!

LIFE PRO TIP *Sometimes we need motivation to help push us to continue to take the necessary steps to reach our goals. We can get stuck, and it can be easier to just give up instead of taking the next step in our journey. It can help to share our goals with other people—by doing so, we make it harder for ourselves to quit because other people will know we quit. Keep yourself in check and let others know about what you want to accomplish so that you have one more reason to continue taking action.*

THINK BIG AND EXPECT MORE

Thinking big means expecting the best outcome and striving to achieve far-reaching goals. If we have modest goals and objectives, we'll likely hit them. But if we have big and audacious goals, even if we don't hit them, we'll likely achieve a lot more than if we had started out with a meager vision. If we're starting a company, then we need to have the goal of being the best company that offers that good or service. If we're starting with a new employer, we should strive to reach the pinnacle levels of the organization, and we should think about the necessary steps we need to take to get there. Don't strive for average goals. We should expect to be massively successful. Will you reach all of your aspirations? Only you can answer that question, but with the right positive mindset, you're setting yourself up for the best chances of success.

It's important to acknowledge that our goals *are* possible and that we *are* able to reach them despite any challenges we might face. Even if we don't reach those goals, just having that vision of ourselves will be hugely impactful in our life. Thinking big isn't just about setting big goals—it's an important part of having a successful mindset. It's knowing that perseverance and hard work will win over talent. It's setting a minimum standard for what we consider acceptable and elevating what we'll accept in both our personal and professional lives.

High standards don't mean that we have to drive a German luxury car. They *do* mean that we're currently driving a dependable car and living in a small apartment but that we're working towards a much bigger lifestyle. It means that we know we are on a road that will lead us to choose to drive an inexpensive, dependable car not because we have to but because we choose to. We are choosing to live a minimalist lifestyle—we're not forced to live that way because we have no wealth.

Raising our standards and thinking big is about having big goals that we simply *must* achieve. These are not goals we'd like to meet, but rather that we simply *must* meet without exception. Make the decision to be more disciplined with your life. Tell yourself that you're not willing to tolerate mediocrity and that the lifestyle you wish to live is more important than anything else. It's not going to be easy! It's hard, and it has to be hard in order for it to be rewarding.

Thinking big also means having clearly written-out goals, goals that you fully believe are possible and achievable and that you measure over time. If your goals relate to your net worth, create a spreadsheet and regularly update it with how you're reducing debts and increasing your assets. But it's not just about money or assets—goals can include spending time with your family or donating your time to charity. It's about balancing your personal life and your professional life. Still, there will be moments in your life when you simply must prioritize one over the other.

Often times, particularly when we're first establishing our goals and starting our journey, we're going to need to focus more on our professional life. That means getting financially fit so that we eventually have the option to spend our free time in any way we want. We have to avoid getting stuck in a debt cycle! Yes, those months and years will be hard—we should acknowledge that truth and brace ourselves for what will be a grind. We have to do the grind in order to have freedom down the road and eventually have options. Isn't it worth it to sacrifice now in order to later reach the standards and goals we *must* have in life?

Let's spend a minute talking about mistakes we have already made in the past or might make in the future. (And mistakes we might avoid making if we have a purpose-driven life.) We *will* make those mistakes, and we *will* learn from them. But we must make sure those mistakes are related to actions that we feel were right in the first place. Mistakes that go against our moral code or are contrary to what we believe in are hard to explain and hard to get over. That's because those really aren't mistakes at all—they're poor decisions. Often those poor decisions take place when we're not taking clear and calculated action. Getting behind the wheel after drinking is an example of a poor decision. The outcomes can range from getting arrested for a DUI to going to prison for accidentally killing someone.

Bad decisions in life happen. The ones that are made with the right intentions in mind aren't really so much poor decisions but rather an action that didn't play out as expected. We can learn from those outcomes. But some bad decisions are bad moral decisions and are made at the expense of our moral compass, like stealing, cheating, or making decisions while under the influence. Bad moral decisions only tear down what we've built and almost always result in an outcome that limits our options. It's okay if you've made bad moral decisions in the past – we have all fallen short at one point in our lives. Just learn from that situation and commit to not repeating that decision.

EMOTIONAL INTELLIGENCE

We all have a pretty good understanding of what's meant by our IQ, or our intelligence quotient. IQ tests measure intellectual abilities and the potential for mental capacity. Emotional intelligence, on the other hand, is the ability to be aware of the dynamics of the relationships we have with different people. It's the ability to both effectively express our emotions while also accounting for the emotions of the people around us. People with high EI can sense how others are feeling and can respond with actions that effectively correspond to the other person. Emotional intelligence is an important concept in both our personal life and our professional career. It's also something we can work on and practice to improve. Fundamentally, EI is about understanding our own emotions as well as the emotions of others.

In our professional life, emotional intelligence is extremely important because a lot of our career success will depend on how well we work with others—we need to be aware of how we are perceived. Being able to stay calm and patient during times of stress will differentiate us from others. Having emotions at work is natural, but it's important to remain calm and never get angry or aggressive. We need to always take the high road, especially if someone we're working with is emotional. The calm person will almost always be viewed as the person who's trying to talk through the challenge in a constructive manner, while the person who gets loud or angry is almost always viewed as being difficult. Right or wrong, that is the perception. So we must always remain calm and remember that one poor response can sink our reputation. And our reputation is one of our most valuable assets!

Our ability to remain professional and confident in difficult situations will be a sign of leadership that many companies will value. As we move up in the organization, we'll be expected to handle ourselves calmly in a professional manner. We should never raise our voices or show anger—doing so will leave a lasting impression. When confronted with difficult situations, it's best to take a deep breath and appreciate the situation for what it is: a moment in time that won't likely matter in the medium to long term. We can't let our reaction to a short-term problem impact our long-term prospects.

Being able to deal with people in a calm and professional manner is expected of a high-performing employee. It's also important to know when we can be ourselves and have casual discussions at work. If we're "client-facing"—meaning we directly interact with customers—it's even more important to work on developing our EI because often times the outcome depends on how you react to what the client is saying. We have to be straightforward when delivering difficult messages but still end the discussion on a positive note. We can find a silver lining and highlight that point so the discussion remains constructive. If we're dealing with customers on a customer service level, we should allow the client to talk and express their concern or issue. Often just venting helps with moving past the problem.

People with a low EI often have difficulty explaining themselves when they're emotional—they can get quickly overwhelmed. People who don't have a handle on their thoughts and emotions often struggle to be assertive and in control. People with a high EI, on the other hand, react in the opposite way. These people often demonstrate an ability to stay calm and collected during moments of stress. They are able to assess a situation and share thoughtful and constructive thoughts on how to improve it. They can take difficult feedback and not react as though it's personal.

The leaders in your organization will likely have a relatively high EI. The ability to lead others also comes along with having a sense of confidence and know-how when dealing with a situation. Most people gravitate to someone who is confident in their delivery and has a clear plan to remedy a situation. It's important to show conviction and confidence when leading a discussion or when leading others.

EI is a powerful concept and one that most successful people either knowingly or unknowingly use to their advantage.

We should take the time to assess our own EI and work on any gaps we self-identify. Improving our own EI can make a huge difference in both our personal and professional lives.

BUILDING A BRAND AT WORK

I'm regularly asked by younger people who are starting their careers about how to be successful at work. "How do you stand out from the crowd?" is a question I often hear. It's a good one! We're about to spend some time discussing a number of both qualitative and quantitative attributes that we should be using to strategically position ourselves in the workplace. We can look at people who are considered to be top performers in their fields and identify common traits that we can replicate ourselves.

Successful people have a solid understanding of their role within the company and are subject matter experts at what they do. At the same time, they're likable people whom others want to interact with. These people are efficient and understand the expectations of their job, in addition to being personable and likable. They ask their manager how they're measured and work to exceed those metrics every day. Aside from having a command of their tasks, people with successful careers also get along with their colleagues and are viewed as someone whom others want to work with. Essentially, they possess two high-level skills: they are efficient, and they have a positive disposition. Many people have one or the other, but having both is what makes a person stand out.

In thinking about how you could stand out from your peers, let's start with the specific tasks of your job. It could be manufacturing a product, dealing with clients, or selling. It could be anything, but each role comes with core expectations that must be met in order for an employee to stay employed. High performers know which skills or outcomes are measured and closely monitor how they are doing against those goals. If you don't know what these metrics are for your role, schedule some time with your manager and ask them what you need to do to be considered a high-performing employee. Ask questions that allow your manager to explain what they view as an "ideal employee." That will typically include showing up on time, being polite to others, staying focused on your tasks, etc. Having and demonstrating these skills means you'll typically meet the bare minimum and will get a "meets expectations" rating, which is enough to keep your job. Once you know what the bare-minimum tasks are, ask what it takes to be a high performer within the company.

Reduce Expenses and Grow Revenue

Once we have a good understanding of the basics and what it takes to stand out, we can use that information to improve how things are currently done within the company. At the end of the day, every company cares about reducing expenses and growing revenue. Thinking of ways to make our job more efficient by evaluating tasks and thinking of ways to conduct those tasks at a lower cost is what will really accelerate our career. Taking an interest in the company and having ideas that reduce costs or increase revenue will be welcomed by our manager and *their* manager. For example, maybe we can eliminate a step in the production cycle, resulting in fewer people being required to finish the task. That will reduce expenses.

We can ask our managers how they themselves are evaluated for success and think about what we can do to help them achieve *their* goals. Being a resource that our manager values and would miss if we left is a great way to differentiate ourselves and become valuable to the company. Every company looks at the cost per employee, and if we're not in sales, then we're a cost. Finding ways to reduce cost is how we stand out. Companies need to find value in what we do that's greater than the cost we are to the company. This isn't always appreciated or understood by employees, but to be blunt, if we aren't adding a value that's equal to our cost, then it's difficult to sustain the role. Yes, some infrastructure jobs (IT staff, administrative assistants, accountants) are pure costs paid for by sales generated by others, but the people in these roles can contribute by finding ways to cut other expenses.

Adding value to the point where our bosses would miss us if we left is what we should strive for. If we're easily replaced by someone else in a matter of hours, then we're not bringing enough to the table to be recognized and ultimately promoted or paid more. Our boss needs to want us as an employee—if they do, they're going to be our advocate.

Exceed Simple Expectations

So, be indispensable! Also, try to exceed simple expectations like showing up on time. Never be late—in fact, come in a little early to see if you can help your boss get things ready for the day. Sign up for overtime. Dress well by investing in clothes that show you're thinking a couple of steps (i.e., jobs) ahead. You can find great second-hand business clothes as an affordable option. Look at how your manager and their manager are dressed and mimic them. If you wear a uniform, this might not be as applicable, but always have it clean and pressed. Be well-groomed.

Whether we like it or not, people unconsciously form opinions based on our appearance. I don't like it, either, but I've learned not to resist. Go with what works most of the time; having a great appearance and presence. If you want to make a statement with your appearance and go against what's traditionally viewed as professional, that's perfectly fine, too. It has worked for some people. On average, though, it's not a great approach. I'm not discouraging you from being unique, but I do want to encourage you to do what works the majority of the time and gives you the highest probability of success. Looking professional is what works most of the time.

Having a command of the skills that are necessary to exceed expectations is core, but we also want to be viewed as a positive and likable person, a person who takes on new tasks, a person who happily does what's necessary to get the job done with quality results. I've found that the single easiest thing to do if you want to be the go-to person is simple: just follow up. Take notes and actually do what you say you'll do. If you're on a project team, keep track of other tasks that you're *not* assigned and ask if you can help.

Follow Through and Be Likable

Unfortunately, many people simply don't follow through with tasks, and eventually, the leadership of a company won't trust them to get things done, and they'll lose their opportunity to advance. It's so important to keep track of what we said we'll do...and then do it! Take notes and keep a running tally of all your outstanding tasks. Keep working on the tasks until they're completed. This holds true for internal follow-up and also when it comes to following up with customers. I'm sure you've been told that a company would do one thing or another, but then it never happened because the employee you spoke with didn't follow through. Don't be one of those people.

Let's also spend some time discussing the likability factor. It's a key attribute that I see time and time again in successful people. On the other hand, I've seen many people be masters at what they do, yet others don't like working with them. If you don't engage with others as part of your job, then this isn't as important, but most of us will interact with others at the workplace.

People enjoy dealing with people they like. Being likable doesn't actually take very much effort, but we do have to make a conscious effort to build rapport with our coworkers. Likable people say, "Good morning!" They say hello to others in the hallway, and they don't gossip about others. (Never trust a person who tells you something that another person told them in confidence – this means that person will do the same to you.) Likable people also take an interest in others and aren't shy—they walk up to people they don't know and introduce themselves.

Introducing ourselves first often sets the tone for that relationship moving forward. We want to be the person who is confident and can walk up to a stranger and say "Hello!" This includes talking to people who are higher up than we are in the organization. Don't be intimidated by people who are senior to you at work! Be respectful, be professional, and respect the role they play within the organization, but also, don't be frightened to say hello just because they're your boss's boss. Those people generally want to interact, but many feel uncomfortable themselves.

Be confident, look people in the eye, and introduce yourself by saying your full name (first and last) and the role you play within the organization. When you meet the same person again, they likely won't remember your name, so say it again if you're having a one-on-one discussion. If your name is Brianna, then just say, "Hey, I'm Brianna Smith. Good to see you again!" They'll remember that they met you in the past, and you just made their life easier by reminding them of your name. Also, try to use the other person's name as much as you can—for example, say good morning using their name. Avoid using slang like "Hey there!" or some other term we often use if we don't know the other person or have forgotten their name.

And don't ignore support staff! Say hello to the boss's administrative assistant and make an effort to build a relationship with that person. That person has a unique dialog with your manager and can help you greatly if they like you as a person. Simply saying hello makes a difference. Say hello to the janitorial staff and the cafeteria staff. Be nice to everyone. People see this and are then nice to you. The key takeaway regarding likability is that while talent will take you places, character and the ability to get along with others are what keep you there.

Be Professional and Confident

I've used the term "confidence," but that means different things to different people. In the context of the workplace, it means being sure of ourselves and speaking in a clear tone. If we're running a meeting, we shouldn't beat around the bush—we need to kick off the meeting and lay out the agenda. This includes presenting to larger audiences as well. We need to tell the crowd what we're going to share in terms of the agenda, cover key agenda topics and then close by recapping what we've told them. For example, we would say, "Today I'm going to review X, Y, and Z," and then proceed to review each item one at a time. When we're done with Z, then we would wrap up the meeting or presentation by saying, "So today we've discussed XYZ. I'm happy to address any questions." Laying out the key points and clearly labeling each one ensures that the audience walks away with what they were supposed to learn.

We want to build our brand of being a smart employee who is hardworking, comes up with helpful ideas, *and* is a good person to work with. Exhibiting all of these skills results in an outcome that's better than if we were to just "wing it." Winging it results in average performance with average results, and we can do better than that.

Take control of how people view you and how they value your brand. Be a go-to person who's dependable and known for getting things done. Introduce yourself and say hi to people. Dress for the job you want, not the job you have—look at the way your boss's boss dresses and acts for cues. Avoid behaviors that can negatively impact the way people perceive you, like drinking too much with your coworkers or discussing activities that might be outside of company policy. (It's generally not a great idea to discuss the partying we did over the weekend or our plans for the next.) In short, be professional at work. That's the easiest way to move up, yet it only takes one bad decision to immediately change how people perceive us. Perception *is* reality, and perceptions of us can change in a minute. And it might take a *lot* of effort to change those back.

Think about ways to develop work relationships and never miss an opportunity to congratulate someone for their success, no matter how small or big it is. People do like and remember that. Just as we need positive influencers who encourage us, we also need to be that person for those around us. People like to engage with uplifting people because doing so makes them feel better. We want people to think positive thoughts when *our* name comes up!

Be proud of your reputation of being on time and always dependable. Don't call out sick unless you're truly ill and are likely to get someone else sick. Avoid taking unplanned days (taking sick days when you're not sick) off work because of an issue in your personal life. Everybody has to deal with personal problems, but it's best not to let personal issues interfere with your employment. And don't say too much during certain situations, especially in writing.

Build a brand that represents loyalty, hard work, and a positive attitude. Ever heard the saying that if you want to get something done, find the busiest person and ask them to do it? That person is typically a can-do and go-to person. Be the go-to person your colleagues think of. Be eager to take on more responsibilities and contribute to projects at work. Raise your hand and ask where you can help. Also, be constructive with your feedback when asked about what can be better in your workplace.

Speak Up in a Thoughtful Way

When you're in team or group meetings, raise your hand and ask a question. Think about your question in advance and even jot it down before you ask it so you're not as nervous. It's okay to read it from your notes—just say something like, "I wrote it down so I wouldn't forget." (Generally, if we acknowledge something that makes us feel embarrassed, then we won't feel self-conscious because we've already acknowledged what others are thinking - taking away their power.) Don't put the speaker on the spot or have a negative tone when you ask a question—stay optimistic and constructive. If you have any negative feedback, convey that on a one-on-one basis, not in a group setting.

Delivering negative feedback without providing helpful suggestions for improvement isn't constructive, either. Remember, the squeaky wheel gets the grease...but the screechy wheel gets replaced.

Sit at the front of the room! Don't go to the back of the room during meetings. Be someone whom the leadership team recognizes. If you sit at the back, you'll get lost in the crowd, and guess what will then happen to your career? It will get lost in the crowd as well. Be confident and show others you can handle the spotlight and compose yourself in front of a crowd. Almost everyone is nervous when public speaking—only a few can compose themselves and appear confident. Having prepared statements written down is really helpful when public speaking. Don't wing it! Public speaking off the cuff can either go very well or very badly, but speaking with prepared comments typically comes across as being mature and is generally viewed as positive or neutral. Even if it's viewed as neutral, people will still remember that you spoke up, which is important. No leader wants to hear crickets when they ask the audience if they have any questions, so be a positive contributor to meetings.

Let's think specifically about situations when we need to make a decision or recommendation at the workplace. When put in this position, it's always good to think about how the decision will impact three parties: 1) the company's shareholders (which is a nice way of saying how the decision might impact the financial results—remember, shareholders own the company), 2) the company's customers, and 3) the company's employees. Every decision needs to balance these three needs. If one of the three parties is going to materially lose, then there needs to be a very good reason to move forward. These three parties are really the groups that add value to or get value out of the company, and considering all three will make us come across as thinking holistically and across the organization. When asked about a decision that's potentially far-reaching, we should lay out our response within the context of how our answer impacts each of the three constituents.

If you have a sensitive topic to discuss, it's much better to send a note and ask to discuss it live rather than go into great detail in writing. Writing makes our thoughts and perceptions (and often misperceptions) permanent and on the record. I know you've heard this before, but don't send any email that has a negative tone or belittles anyone. Never write an angry email and hit "send"! Don't send an email until you've cooled down and slept on it overnight. If you have to address a time-sensitive situation immediately, ask to speak live.

If you do actually have to send an email, make sure you have all of your facts straight and can provide a fact-based email response, not an emotional email. Also, note that no one wants to get a three- or four- or five-paragraph email. Think about the key points and make them into easy-to-digest bullets with comments that get right to the point. Long paragraphs are often not read, so making the email "punchy" is much more likely to make an impact. If you have a very lengthy subject to discuss, ask to speak live, but if you're still asked to put it in an email, then go for it! You know the recipient is okay with reading a novel. Just use bullets as much as possible.

LIFE PRO TIP *Draft the subject and body of the email and have it ready to send prior to adding recipients. Don't put people on the 'To:' line until the email is completely written out. Too often, emails are accidentally sent in draft form, and waiting until the end takes that risk off the table.*

Own Your Mistakes and Be Helpful

We want to be viewed as a person with integrity and a person who owns their mistakes. We shouldn't come up with excuses, particularly if we did something wrong and the mistake is on us. The outcome will be much better if we own it and simply state, "I could have done a better job at X, Y and Z." We shouldn't be afraid to say, "I take responsibility here—I could have done X, Y and Z better." The leadership team will be much more impressed with our maturity and honesty than they will be disappointed that we made a mistake.

Blaming others is a sure fire way to lose people's respect. Making mistakes that we originally felt were the right thing isn't how we lose the trust or respect of others—on the contrary, picking ourselves up after the mistake and owning it is how we build a strong reputation. Leaders are chosen because they are a working example of how the company wants its employees to behave. They represent the values of the company, and being trustworthy and owning our actions are values that every company puts high on its list of priorities.

It's quite important to build a good and positive relationship with our direct manager. We want that individual to genuinely like us as a person. Being respectful of our direct manager goes a really long way, because they want to feel respected and feel as though they deserve the role. Most people want approval from others, and that includes wanting approval from the people who work for them. We never want to belittle our manager in any setting. Our manager is the one who's going to write our performance review and can help with the promotion we might be striving for.

We also should focus on being nice and helpful and adding value to team meetings by contributing and speaking up. No manager wants a silent meeting where they feel like they have to extract interactions from the team. We can help facilitate successful meetings for our managers! Managers deal with all types of employees, and many people can be quite challenging.

Be one of the easy-to-deal-with employees. And by the way, once we become managers ourselves, we should avoid awkward meetings by assigning a different team member to be the meeting host each week—that way, someone new is running each meeting. We'll get engaged employees because the team will feel vested in the meetings.

Get Things Done

We should avoid saying we do not have time to do something. Instead, we can share that we have a number of priorities but that we're certainly willing to take on more. This is the kind of attitude people want to hear and see in the workplace. We should always take on more responsibilities if we're asked to do so...or we should be prepared to be passed up when there's another opportunity down the road.

That said, we might actually begin to get overloaded at some point. If that happens, then we should simply go to our manager and ask for guidance regarding prioritizing. This is a much better approach than saying "No" or "I don't have enough time." We should be willing to take on more, but we should also understand that our time will need to be prioritized by the organization. The bottom line is that everyone has 24 hours per day, including the most successful people we know. Successful people don't focus on not being able to do something because they don't have time—they think about how they can prioritize to get things done, and they welcome new challenges. Successful people know that putting in the effort is key. They don't turn down new opportunities because they think they don't have time.

It's also important to find a small group at work—our own network—of trusted partners who can help us navigate the organization. Some of these trusted colleagues will be senior to us; some will be peers; others might be junior to us. It's important to respect the levels of the organization. We absolutely should not share what senior people have shared with us with others—if we're trusted enough to have information that others don't have, we shouldn't wreck that trust. Sharing sensitive information is a quick way to damage how others perceive us.

The brand we develop is fully within our control. We own our reactions to situations, how hard we work, and whether we're confident enough to stand out amongst our peers. None of the strategies we've discussed are difficult—in fact, they're commonly understood. But they're not commonly practiced. Be a person who puts these strategies in place and purposefully owns and navigates their career!

> **LIFE PRO TIP** *We've discussed that a company will pay us based on the value we bring to the company, but there's another variable companies use when evaluating compensation: how the market might value our contributions. It's important for our employer to understand that we're marketable and that if we're not treated fairly (in terms of compensation, benefits, paid time off, etc.), we have options. We can find another role if it comes down to it. Now, we're not saying we'll leave if we don't get this or that. Threatening to leave the company is like pulling out a gun—if you pull it out, you better be ready to use it. But it does mean we should stay active in understanding our options outside of our employer. Whether we like it or not, many companies will pay us just enough for us not to leave. If we give the perception that the risk of leaving is essentially zero, then we may be compensated as such.*

VARIOUS DEGREES OF SUCCESS

All of the core concepts we've discussed so far can work in conjunction with each other to greatly improve our chances of achieving our definition of success. These strategies can greatly improve our chances of living a purpose-driven and fulfilling life! Small advantages add up over time and have an accumulative beneficial effect.

Let's take a moment and discuss how we typically think of success. While there's a wide range of opinions regarding what "success" is, people typically value these three forms of success:

1. Emotional/relationship success
2. Personal achievement success
3. Financial success

Emotional success is a common (and often subconscious) goal that many of us share. This means feeling fulfilled by personal relationships we have with family members or friends or our partner. Most importantly, we want to feel fulfilled within ourselves. This topic is very personal and is measured very differently from one person to the next. Our view of success isn't likely what everyone else views as success.

Say we have someone who prioritizes their career over having a traditional family and, as a result, is financially successful. They are happy with what they've accomplished. A mother who makes less money and has two beloved children might feel sorry for that person. Her definition of "success" is just as accurate. At the end of the day, each of us has our own personal view of success, and that's perfectly okay. We just need to be aware of this and respect the choices and goals of others.

Personal achievement success can cover a wide spectrum of goals, but what we're really referencing here is having the goal of getting good at (or even being the best at) a specific task or process. It could be learning a new skill, like skiing or cooking, or learning a new language. It could be joining a local bowling league or winning trivia nights. Personal achievement success is important to celebrate and continue to work on because these gradual improvements add to our overall satisfaction in life.

Think of hobbies or activities that interest you and set goals you want to achieve. Maybe you've always wanted to learn woodworking, or you've always wanted to learn how to skateboard.

Don't put off these goals and opportunities for success! Life is *now*, and thinking that you'll get around to doing something "one day" is dangerous. Go out and start getting involved and doing the things that excite you now.

Financial success generally means we have access to sufficient income that enables us to fund our desired lifestyle. Financial success is monetary-based, and financial goals evolve over time—one person's early view of financial success might be paying down debt, while another person might be close to their lifelong goal of achieving financial independence. Both are based on improving our personal balance sheet and maximizing our income just like a well-run company does.

It's important not to be intimidated or discouraged when comparing our success to the successes of others. In fact, we shouldn't even *be* comparing ourselves to others—we should be comparing our current success level to our own success level from a year ago. While it's important to learn from people who are ahead of us, at the same time, we shouldn't be discouraged. We should have relationships with these people so that we can bounce ideas off of them. People who have achieved the goals we've set for ourselves might be wiser than us because they simply have more life experiences than we do.

Being in Good Company

Remember, we want to associate ourselves with people who share our goals and encourage us to take measured risks. Some people won't be there for us as we reach for various levels of success. Some will even detract us from our goals. We need to spend time with people who encourage us rather than spend time with people who bring challenges and drama. In order to succeed, we need to make the tough call and decide who's in our circle and who's toxic to our success. Toxic people gossip and belittle people who go after their dreams and fail. Toxic people enjoy watching others fail, either secretly or openly.

Over time, we'll be able to identify people who are and aren't going to be helpful in our journey. We need to be surrounded by people who encourage us to keep going and who support us after we've failed. These are the influencers we want in our life. We can get to know people who invest and who are interested in talking about the market and sharing different financial concepts. Plenty of people are happy to discuss personal finance!

There's a phrase: "If you're the smartest person in your group, then you better find a new group." We want a team of people we can learn from and seek guidance and counsel from. This group will form over time. Typically, it includes friends or acquaintances who are more experienced than we are and who help us avoid mistakes. (This could be a chat group of like-minded users, for example.) As our investment horizons grow, we will add other professional team members, like accountants, lawyers, property management companies, realtors, investment managers, banking partners, etc. All of those are examples of having a well-rounded team.

Now, we might think that's way out of our grasp. I used to think so, too, but it all goes back to having a big goal and then thinking about the very next step we need to take to achieve that goal. Any goal you might have is possible – you have to genuinely believe that. Don't get hung up on how long it might take to get there—just understand that it's possible for you to take action. Do that step and then think about the very next step. Do *that* step and then think about the very next step... You get the idea. Don't discourage yourself and think that these are only dreams. They will be your reality one day if you believe they're possible and you take the very next step to reach your goal.

This guide has outlined many of the key concepts all of us need to understand in order to greatly improve our chances of financial success. My hope is that you'll use these concepts to map out your own unique plan for attaining personal achievements as well as an emotionally fulfilling life. Financial success might not make problems entirely go away, but it's a lot easier to solve life's challenges with financial security than without it.

If you had to choose between being financially secure versus financially struggling, I'm guessing you would go ahead and take the advantages that financial success provides.

AP Adulting Concepts

If you're reading this and have already graduated from school (high school or college), then you're already an adult. This chapter is designed to enhance your knowledge of topics that impact us as adults, either directly or indirectly. The subject matter might not be required for adults to understand but having a high-level understanding of the concepts is quite important if you want to have an advantage over others. Sure, you can get by without this knowledge, but a working understanding of taxes or our monetary system just makes you a more well-rounded person. It also helps you avoid mistakes made through trial and error and learning these subjects the hard way like many of us do.

Most people learn these concepts over time through life experiences. You won't find these subjects in most textbooks. This section was specifically designed to identify topics that formal education doesn't typically cover. Take the time to read and understand these topics so that when (not if) you experience the subject, you're comfortable with the concepts and can make more intelligent and educated decisions. I'll warn you now, though, that this is Advanced Placement content, so take your time and re-read passages if necessary. It will be worth the effort.

HOW MONEY WORKS

A half-century ago, the US was on what's called the "gold standard," meaning that every dollar in circulation could be redeemed for physical gold. This generally kept inflation low because the money supply was limited to the amount of gold that the US Federal Reserve held in their vault. In 1971, that all changed when President Richard Nixon halted the convertibility of dollars to gold. Then, in 1973, the president officially eliminated the gold standard altogether. Once that happened, the Federal Reserve could print money at will and not have to worry about physical gold backing the dollar. When the dollar went off the gold standard, it became what's referred to as a fiat currency. A fiat currency is a government-issued currency that's not backed by a physical asset such as gold or silver. Fiat currency can just simply be printed. Although we did have systematic challenges while on the gold standard such as bank runs (people fearfully withdrawing all their funds), this change in going off the gold standard had a number of implications, including inflation.

Essentially, inflation happens when too much money is chasing too few goods. In practical terms, inflation is a steady increase in the prices of the goods we purchase. The US uses what's called the Consumer Price Index, or CPI, to track inflation. CPI measures what's called a "basket of goods" that includes (but is not limited to) food and beverages, housing, clothing, transportation, education costs, and medical care costs. The prices are tracked over time, and the increase in the prices of these goods over time is generally what's viewed as inflation. Maintaining inflation at around 2% each year and ensuring maximum (sustainable) employment are the two primary goals of the Federal Reserve.

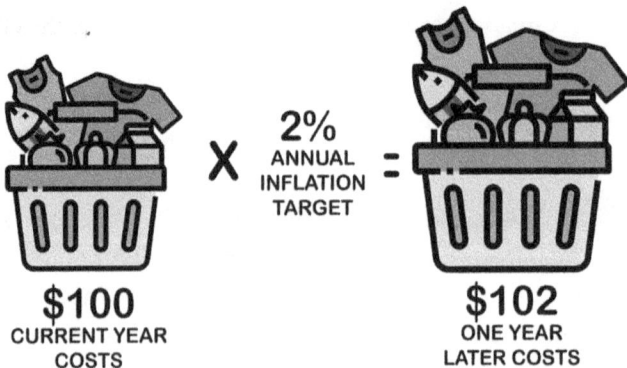

$100
CURRENT YEAR
COSTS

X **2%** ANNUAL INFLATION TARGET =

$102
ONE YEAR
LATER COSTS

Let's spend some time discussing the Federal Reserve and what they do. You'll hear the Federal Reserve referred to as "the Fed." The Fed is an independent group that reports to and is chartered by Congress but is in fact made up of private banks. Member banks hold stock (ownership shares) in the Federal Reserve. These banks include the large banks we see across the US: JPMorgan Chase & Co., Bank of America Corporation, and Citibank, amongst others. The Fed is accountable to Congress and oversees what's referred to as "US monetary policy." Monetary policy is simply the oversight of both the short-term borrowing interest rate (often overnight borrowing between banks) and the money supply. The objective is to use these two tools to ensure price stability (making sure inflation is around 2%) and low unemployment through economic growth. The Fed can change the supply of money by leveraging available tools such as either increasing or decreasing short-term interest rates.

When the Fed *raises* interest rates, the cost of debt to consumers goes up. That means consumers are less likely to spend and run up debt due to the higher cost of borrowing. Large multinational corporations will also issue less debt because it's too expensive, so their spending might also reduce because they have less cash on hand. All this reduction in spending means less demand for goods. Less demand for goods will eventually reduce prices for goods because fewer people are buying them. Increasing interest rates also reduces the money supply because banks are more likely to leave cash with the Federal Reserve because of more attractive interest rates (because rates were increased). Banks make more money when their cash sits with the Fed, and this in turn reduces the amount of money in the economy by lowering the money supply. The Fed can also use its own balance sheet to sell assets (like US Treasuries which is a US dept), which puts more cash into the Fed's balance sheet (moving from holding Treasuries to holding cash), which in turn reduces the money supply because that money (cash) is now within the Fed. More money with the Fed means less money circulating in the economy, which in turn makes money more expensive because there is less of it. Less money in the system makes the money that remains in the system more expensive, which also raises rates.

When the Fed *lowers* interest rates, the cost of debt to consumers goes down. That means consumers are more likely to spend because money is "cheap"—it's inexpensive to borrow debt because rates are low. People might borrow from their home equity because the borrowing costs are low. Large multinational corporations will issue more debt because debt is cheaper. Because there are more loans, more of the money supply is outside of the Federal Reserve, so the money supply also increases when interest rates are low. You might hear that the Fed is "printing money." What they are actually doing is lowering interest rates (which increases the money supply). If the Fed keeps rates too low for too long, inflation will start to increase, and goods will eventually become more and more expensive. Because reversing inflation is quite challenging once it starts, the Fed is incredibly careful with how long it keeps rates low. The Fed can also use their own massive balance sheet to purchase assets (like US Treasuries) which puts more cash in the economy and makes the cash less valuable (because there's more of it), which reduces rates.

The Fed has a number of other tools to manage inflation by managing the money supply—there's a lot more to read if you search "Federal Reserve tools." The key here is to have a conceptual understanding of the Fed's role and how it manages the money supply up or down. Generally, the Fed will keep rates low when the economy is in trouble and will gradually increase rates when the economy is hot and employment is low so that inflation doesn't creep. It's a balancing act that the Fed must manage.

The other set of tools that the government uses to improve a challenging economy is fiscal policy. Fiscal policy uses government spending on new infrastructure programs such as new interstate highways. More government spending circulates more dollars in the economy and creates jobs. Fiscal policy is used by the US Government, while monetary policy is used by the Fed.

A minute on Fiscal policy. The US Government has the capacity to issue bonds (debt) and borrow unimaginable amounts of money, which leads to balance deficits. If the government wants to build a new railway system or fund a defense department project, it issues bonds (debt). All of these deficits build up year after year, resulting in an overall "National Debt." As of this writing, our US National Debt stands at $30 Trillion. There are about 330,000,000 US citizens, meaning that each citizen (including children) owes about $90,000 in National Debt.

HOW CREDIT SCORES WORK

Your credit score is used by individuals or companies or banks when they are making a decision that involves your creditworthiness. The higher your credit score is, the more history you have of paying your debts on time and eventually paying in full without default. The credit score looks at a number of factors when evaluating an individual score: 1) payment history, 2) total amount of actual debt versus what's available to you to borrow, 3) credit history and track record over time, 4) types of credit, and 5) new credit inquiries against your credit profile.

Experian, Equifax Inc., and TransUnion are all credit agencies within the US. These private companies offer their services to creditors (banks, landlords, etc.) for a fee. The three agencies all generally work the same way and evaluate the same criteria. Some creditors will "pull" all three of the agencies' reports, while some may only pull one or two. Your individual score is typically very similar for each agency unless there's an error in reporting, in which case you can open up an investigation into that individual agency to rectify the error.

Payment History

The five metrics that these three agencies review make sense when you think about each one of them individually. Payment history looks at the extent to which you've paid your bills on time. Banks and other creditors will report late payments (over 30 days late) to the credit agencies, and the agencies will then lower your score. It's really important to pay your bills on time so that you don't have late fees show up on your credit report. Having a good payment history without late fees is critical to having a high credit score. If you are late with your payment, you can call the credit card company and likely have the fee waived, but this only works one time.

Your Debt vs. What You Can Borrow

The total amount you owe versus what you can borrow is pretty self-explanatory. Your credit score will be higher if you have, for example, a total of $10,000 in credit but only $2,000 used (meaning you have $8,000 in credit that you haven't used) versus having used $9,500 of the $10,000 (meaning you only have $500 left to use). The ratio of credit use (outstanding) to credit available is basically how this is measured. Avoid going over 50% of your available credit. If you have $10,000 in available credit, don't go over $5,000 in utilized credit.

You're less of a credit risk if you have $10,000 available and you never really need it or you used very little of it, either by paying off the full amount due each month or by keeping your balance low. The total amount owed also looks at the total credit you have versus your income. If you make $70,000 per year and you have $30,000 in credit available, then you're likely to have an issue if you apply for another credit card, because you already have enough credit available versus the income you have to pay back your debts. Put differently, the total amount of credit lines versus your total income is also assessed. Bottom line: you want to avoid carrying large balances that result in a high ratio of utilization to total credit. Again, keep this ratio well below 50%.

Credit History

Your credit history evaluates how long you've had credit. The longer you've managed your credit in a smart way, the higher your score will be. If you're right out of school and only have 6 months of on-time payments, your score won't be as high as someone who's been working for 6 years and also has a perfect payment history.

Types of Credit

The types of credit that are taken out are also evaluated because each credit type carries a different risk for creditors. Installment credit lines are lines that have a set number of payments, each with a specific amount that has to be paid each month. That amount typically doesn't change. Examples include a mortgage or a car loan where you took the loan out for X number of years and you pay a specific amount every month until it's paid in full. The other type of credit is revolving credit. Revolving credit has a total credit line amount, but the amount owed at each payment cycle changes each month. An example is credit card debt. Your spending goes up and down each month, and when you pay it back, that opens up available credit for you to use at a later time.

Installment loan amounts go down each month as the payments are made, and you can't withdraw or use the credit on an ongoing basis—the loan amount is set at the beginning and you pay it down over time. Revolving credit lines allow users to use the line and then pay it back so that they can borrow again against the line. For example, if you have a revolving credit line (say a credit card) of $100 and you use $75 throughout the month, you can pay off the $75 at the end of the month and have the full $100 to use the next.

Revolving credit is typically viewed as higher-risk credit because whereas a credit agency can predict the monthly amounts owned for installment loans, revolving loans go up and down in amount, and it's more challenging to predict the future status of that loan. A creditor might provide a new loan because your installment and revolving line payments are low when the credit decision is made, but 2 months later, if you lose your job, you might start to run up debt on your revolving line, making your payment-to-income ratio go up. That means you're now riskier. In contrast, the installment line repayment amount was clearly understood when the credit decision was made because it's always the same amount.

We spoke elsewhere in the guide about credit cards versus charge cards. Both are revolving lines, but the charge card is less risky because it must be paid back each month. The credit card, however, can carry a balance.

New Credit

The last metric is new credit. As you apply for new credit (that could be a new credit card, a new car loan, or a lease for a new apartment), your credit score is "pulled." That means credit agencies know you're seeking more credit. This is a risk to creditors because it shows that you're about to increase your debt. The other creditors that already have credit lines out to you are then at more risk because the new credit pull will likely result in additional debt.

There are two types of credit pulls: "soft" and "hard." A soft inquiry is when someone views your credit report for non-lending purposes (like a landlord or employer) or when a lender provides preapproval for a loan (like when you're purchasing a home). Sometimes when you're purchasing a home, you need to show that you prequalify for the mortgage amount of the home because some sellers only want to deal with prequalified home buyers. A hard inquiry is when you're actually applying for a credit card, a mortgage, or an auto loan. At that point, you're officially requesting a line of credit. Soft inquiries don't impact your score, but hard inquiries do impact your score and will stay on your report for 2 years. After that, the hard inquiry goes away.

What Can Drive Down Your Credit Score

Negative factors that drive down your credit score stay with your credit for different amounts of time. As stated above, hard credit pulls last for 2 years. Missed payments, collections accounts (meaning your debt was sold to another creditor as nonperforming debt), and bankruptcies last for 7 years and are dropped after that time. Closed accounts in good standing stay for 10 years. An example of that would be a credit card account with a zero balance that you chose to close. (Maybe you closed it because you didn't want or need the card.) Open accounts in good standing will stay on your report indefinitely.

It should be noted that your credit score will be impacted if you're a co-signer on another person's debt or if you're an authorized user on another person's credit card. An authorized user is a person who's on a credit card account and who typically has a card in their name but is not the primary cardholder. An example might be where your parents have a credit card and they added you to their account—you get a card and can make purchases, but the primary cardholder is someone else. Being an authorized user is tricky because different lenders may or may not report authorized users to the bureaus. Bottom line, you only want to be added as an authorized user if you're sure that the primary borrower is responsible with their credit. To be clear, though, the authorized user is not financially responsible for the primary cardholder's debt. The reporting to the agency is to provide the full picture of available credit that an individual has available.

Don't be confused by an authorized user versus a co-signer. Being a co-signer is exactly the same as taking the credit out on your own. If you have student loan debt and your parents co-signed for it, then they are just as responsible for the debt as you are. Co-signers *are* signing up for the debt obligation; authorized users are *not* legally held accountable for the debt. Never agree to be a co-signer unless you're willing to take on the debt up front. In your mind, you should be prepared to pay back the debt if you're a co-signer because, as a co-signer, you are just as legally responsible for the debt as the primary borrower is. Co-signers are often used to allow the primary borrower to get a loan to perhaps start to generate a credit history of their own.

How to Build and Improve Your Credit

Let's spend a minute discussing how to build and improve your credit. You start with finding a credit card that allows you to pay it off each month without interest and without a fee. The credit line can be low—that's okay. You simply need to use the card over time and pay off the balance each month and never miss a payment. Over time, your credit score will build as you build your credit history of on-time payments. You'll start to see a gradual credit score improvement after 6 months of on-time payments. You can also increase your credit lines over time so that you're using a lower percentage of the total line. Don't use the card more and spend more after the credit increase! You want to use that increase as a way to lower your credit utilization. Also, history is important, so if you have a card and don't use it, then just leave the account open and don't use the card. In fact, destroy the actual plastic. Just have the unutilized credit limit sit there and improve your overall utilization—it will make your rate of utilization lower because then the total amount of your available credit is higher.

Credit scores are really important! Having a low score is very costly for people who don't understand them because having a low credit score means your interest rate will be higher. Low credit scores also keep people from getting mortgages and building wealth through leverage. People with poor credit scores have a hard time renting apartments or getting employed at jobs that require the handling of cash. You're considered riskier to your employer because you might be tempted to steal if you're heavily in debt. (At least, that's the reasoning.) All of this means that working on building a good credit score at a young age will be helpful throughout your life.

A good credit score is a reflection of how you handle your priorities. It can be viewed as an extension of your reputation or brand, so build and guard your score with pride. The score sticks with you for life.

690 - 719
GOOD

300 - 629
BAD

720 - 850
EXCELLENT

LIFE PRO TIP We've heard this before: "It's never a good idea to mix business and pleasure." That's very true! Lending money to friends and relatives often times results in a bad outcome. The borrower might not pay us back, or they might be late with their payments because they feel there won't be any real repercussions for doing so. This isn't the case for everyone, clearly, but it's more common than you'd think.

If you decide to get financially involved with friends and family, it's better to **treat it as a gift** and not have any strings attached in terms of repayment. The friend or family member can certainly pay you back if they want to, but having a time-

line with payment amounts in place almost always plays out badly and can ruin relationships. If you want to help someone out and don't want to risk losing a friend, give them a gift. Or have a hardline approach to never lending to friends and family. Same goes for giving financial advice—friends and family don't typically react well to this because it's mixing business and pleasure.

HOW TAXES WORK

This is another detail-heavy subject where the Advanced Placement nature of this book will come through. You might even want to review this section again to fully grasp the concepts/examples.

First, let's have a quick discussion about how US federal taxes work. US federal taxes are deeply nuanced, so we're just going to generally discuss how income is taxed. This section is not intended to provide any tax advice or guidance—it's just meant to provide conceptual themes.

The US has what is referred to as a "progressive tax system." This means there are various taxable income brackets, where each bracket has a designated tax rate. Because these tax rates and income brackets evolve over time and can change as different political administrations take power, I'm going to use some directional figures to share the concept. (These figures are based on tax brackets in 2021.)

The code has different taxable income brackets with different rates. For example, the first bracket is taxable income from $0 to $10,000, and the tax rate for that bracket is 10%. This means that if you earn $50,000 in taxable income, the first $10,000 will be taxed at 10%. That covers the first $10,000, but you still have another $40,000 of your total $50,000 salary. The tax brackets start to jump materially as you move up the income scale.

The second bracket is income from $10,000 to $40,000 at a rate of $12%. That means that the first $0 to $10,000 is taxed at 10% using the first tax bracket, and the next $10,000 to $40,000 is taxed at 12%. You'll pay taxes on $30,000 ($40,000 minus $10,000) at a rate of 12%. That's $3,600 in taxes within that bracket.

You then have the last $10,000 left to get to your total $50,000 in taxable income because tax brackets 1 and 2 handled the first $40,000. The third bracket goes up once again to cover income from $40,000 to $85,000. This is taxed at a rate of 22%, so you will pay $2,200 for that last $10,000. ($10,000 x 22% = $2,200). Your total tax bill will be $1,000 (from the first bracket) plus $3,600 (from the second bracket) plus $2,200 (for the third bracket). That totals $6,800. Your overall tax rate would be $6,800 / $50,000 = 13%.

EXAMPLE:
$50,000
TAXABLE INCOME

TAX RATE	TAXABLE INCOME BRACKETS		MATH	AMOUNT TAXED
10%	-	$10,000	10% x $10,000	$1,000
12%	$10,000	$40,000	12% x $30,000	$3,600
22%	$40,000	$85,500	22% x $10,000	$2,200
24%	$85,500	$160,000	NOT APPLICABLE	NOT APPLICABLE
32%	$160,000	$210,000	NOT APPLICABLE	NOT APPLICABLE
35%	$210,000	$515,000	NOT APPLICABLE	NOT APPLICABLE
37%	$515,000	+	NOT APPLICABLE	NOT APPLICABLE

TOTAL $6,800

With a progressive tax rate, your income is chopped up into tax brackets and is taxed at higher rates as you move up into each tax bracket. As of the time of this book, there are 7 total brackets where the seventh bracket is taxed at 37% for income that's approximately over $515,000. So, if you have a taxable income of $600,000, then only the last $85,000 is taxed at around 37%. The entire $600,000 isn't taxed at that rate. The first $515,000 is broken down into the other 6 buckets and taxed at rates starting at around 10% (which we discussed above) and then is slowly taxed more as it moves up to the seventh bracket. Let's say you do have a taxable income (for example) of $600,000:

EXAMPLE:
$600,000
TAXABLE INCOME

TAX RATE	TAXABLE INCOME BRACKETS		MATH	AMOUNT TAXED
10%	-	$10,000	10% x $10,000	$1,000
12%	$10,000	$40,000	12% x $30,000	$3,600
22%	$40,000	$85,500	22% x $45,500	$10,010
24%	$85,500	$160,000	24% x $74,500	$17,880
32%	$160,000	$210,000	32% x $50,000	$16,000
35%	$210,000	$515,000	35% x $305,000	$106,750
37%	$515,000	+	37% x $85,000	$31,450

TOTAL $186,690

Taxable income can be reduced by taking advantage of tax-friendly options like contributing to tax-deductible retirement plans or charitable organizations. Think back to the 401k contribution example, where we reduced our taxable income of $50,000 by contributing $1,500 to our 401k. That made our new taxable income $48,500. This is also how other tax-deductible events are handled—they reduce our taxable income. If you have a child, you can take the child tax credit of around $3,000. To continue our example, then your taxable income would go from the original $50,000 to $45,500—you would deduct the $1,500 you contribute to your 401k as well as the $3,000 child tax credit.

Understanding deductions is important because they reduce our tax burden at the higher brackets, the ones that come along with a higher tax rate. In our example, you would have paid taxes of 22% for the third bracket ($40,000 to $85,000), but with your tax deductions, you're paying the 22% rate, not on a full $10,000 but rather on just $5,500 because your taxable income is then $45,500 rather than $50,000. Your tax bill for that third bracket goes down from $2,200 to $1,210.

EXAMPLE:
$50,000
TAXABLE INCOME

TAX RATE	TAXABLE INCOME BRACKETS		BEFORE DEDUCTIONS MATH	BEFORE DEDUCTIONS AMOUNT TAXED	AFTER DEDUCTIONS MATH	AFTER DEDUCTIONS AMOUNT TAXED
10%	-	$10,000	10% x $10,000	$1,000	10% x $10,000	$ 1,000
12%	$10,000	$40,000	12% x $30,000	$3,600	12% x $30,000	$3,600
22%	$40,000	$85,500	22% x $10,000	$2,200	22% x $500	$110
24%	$85,500	$160,000	NOT APPLICABLE	NOT APPLICABLE	NOT APPLICABLE	NOT APPLICABLE
32%	$160,000	$210,000	NOT APPLICABLE	NOT APPLICABLE	NOT APPLICABLE	NOT APPLICABLE
35%	$210,000	$515,000	NOT APPLICABLE	NOT APPLICABLE	NOT APPLICABLE	NOT APPLICABLE
37%	$515,000	+	NOT APPLICABLE	NOT APPLICABLE	NOT APPLICABLE	NOT APPLICABLE
				TOTAL $6,800		TOTAL $4,710

$2,090
LESS IN TAXES

Another common tax deduction is the mortgage interest payments on your primary residence. If you have a $100,000 mortgage and pay an interest rate of 5% on the mortgage loan, you can likely deduct that $5,000 in interest ($100,000 x 5%) from your taxable income in the form of an interest expense deduction. If your taxable income is $50,000 per year and you're a single filer (not married), the amount of your income from $40,000 to $50,000 is assessed at 22%. With an income of $50,000, you'd pay $2,200 in taxes for this bracket ($10,000 x 22%), but if you have $5,000 in interest expenses related to your mortgage, then your taxable income is reduced by that amount. That means your taxable income goes from $50,000 down to $45,000. You now pay that 22% on $45,000 rather than $50,000. That makes your taxes in that tax bracket $1,100 ($5,000 x 22%) rather than $2,200. The mortgage interest expense tax deduction is a way for the government to encourage home ownership.

Let's put all of these examples together: the 401k contribution of $1,500, a child tax credit of $3,000, and an interest expense deduction of $5,000. That's a total of $9,500 in deductions from an income of $50,000. Here's what the tax math looks like:

The third bracket's taxable income went from $10,000 down to $500 because you deducted $9,500 from that bracket ($10,000 minus $9,500 = $500). So, your federal taxes go from $6,800 down to $4,710. That's $2,090 less in taxes because of the 401k contribution, the child tax credit, and the mortgage interest expense. These deductions reduce the amount of taxable income in the highest bracket.

This is how tax deductions work: they reduce our taxable income within the highest bracket we're in. We still pay taxes on our income at varying rates for the lower brackets, but because the amount of our income in the highest bracket is reduced, we get the benefit of reducing the income that carries the highest tax burden. It becomes clearer, why the wealthy love tax breaks—the benefit they receive is often a reduction in taxable income at a rate of 37% (or whatever the highest bracket is at the time you're reading this passage). It's why having tax-friendly savings accounts and starting businesses that reduce their tax burden is how savvy people abide by the tax code while embracing tax benefits that are perfectly legal.

The last point regarding taxes is how they're actually filed. Our employer provides us with a W-2 form which is then used to fill out the appropriate IRS tax form. We'll discuss the W-2 in the upcoming sections, but for now, just know that it's a tax document given to us by our employer outlining all the taxes that we have been paid throughout the year. The vast majority of us will file a Form 1040 – US Individual Income Tax Return. We can really do this ourselves—it's very straightforward and only really requires that we have our W-2 in front of us so we have the various data points. The form will ask that we input specific numbers from the W-2. Everything is very easy to match, and Form 1040 clearly tells us which numbers from the W-2 to put into each field. As our personal financial situations evolve, we might need to start filing out various schedules that are added to Form 1040, but most of us will still only need Form 1040. The schedules are added to Form 1040 and are used when we have deductions like mortgage interest deductions or student loan interest deductions. Most readers will use the Standard Deduction if we don't have specific "itemized" deductions. Itemized deductions are things like mortgage interest deductions. The Standard Deduction is an amount that we can deduct from our earned income if we don't have itemized deductions. You can see what the Standard Deduction is via a simple search for 'US Tax Standard Deduction.' These tax forms and schedules aren't difficult to fill out via online guided templates.

Once we fill out the forms, we file with the IRS by simply submitting through www.IRS.gov. In fact, the IRS website allows us to fill in the forms directly and submit our taxes online. The finished Form 1040 will tell us whether we owe or whether we will get a refund, so we'll know this before we actually file with the IRS. The amount we owe or receive depends on whether our actual tax burden is more than or less than what our employer has deducted via payroll deductions.

Payroll deductions are tied to the number of dependents we have claimed with our employer. If we have one child, we have one dependent; if we have two children, we have two dependents. We just need to notify our employer of how many dependents we have. If we claim two dependents, then our employer will take less out in federal taxes than if we claim one or zero dependents. If we claim two but really have zero, then we need to be prepared to owe taxes at the end of the year because the more dependents we claim, the less our employer takes out. If the number of dependents we claim to have is greater than what we actually claim on our Form 1040, then we will owe more in federal taxes. HR representatives can give us more information regarding dependents, but basically, it's best to claim the true number of children we actually have in our household.

I should also point out that those that are self-employed (business owners / gig workers / etc.) will need to set aside funds throughout the year to pay their tax bill, which is typically paid quarterly. There is no employer HR department that deducts taxes throughout the year, so we have to do that ourselves. You can use online tax calculators to estimate your quarterly amount owed. Be sure to account for this expense throughout the year so you have the necessary accumulated cash saved each quarter to pay your taxes. Don't be like so many that are surprised with a tax bill at the end of their first tax year of being self-employed!

LIFE PRO TIP *The inheritance tax and the gift tax might be applicable to some readers. The gift tax in particular is often misunderstood, but it's actually quite simple. It's related to both inheritance and general gifts given between two individuals. Many people think that if they give a gift that's above a specific annual amount, that amount is taxed, but that isn't correct. We don't need to report a gift to the IRS if an annual gift is less than*

$15,000. If the gift is greater than $15,000 in one year, we need to report it to the IRS so they can keep track of the total amount exchanged between two individuals. The gift tax is only applicable when the total aggregate amount gifted exceeds $11.6 million in a lifetime. That means, as of the time this guide was written, our parents can give us up to $11.6 million without tax implications.

The $15,000-per-year rule is so the government can keep track of the amount of gifts given against the $11.6 million lifetime gift amount. Again, even though you must report the gift to the IRS, if it exceeds $15,000 in a single year, no taxes are paid until all of the gifts add up to $11.6 million over a lifetime. You could receive the whole $11.6 million in one year and there would be no tax penalties. Once you have received more than $11.6 million, however—either in one year or in a lifetime—then there are tax implications.

I hope you face this $11.6 million lifetime gift issue in your life! But whether you ever receive that much, many of you might receive $15,000 (or more) as a gift in any given year, so it's good to have this knowledge.

Paycheck Deductions

Our paycheck will come either weekly, biweekly (every other week), or monthly. We obviously need to have a good budget with specific buckets to pay for expenses if we're paid monthly because that paycheck has to last all month. But even if we're paid weekly, we'll need to do the math on how much we need to accrue (save) each week so that we can pay our monthly bills: rent, utilities, mobile phone, car insurance, etc. Each pay period, we'll have a number of different deductions from our gross pay. The net amount is our take-home pay. Take-home pay is basically our total pay minus taxes, health insurance premiums, Social Security, and Medicare payments, etc. We'll also have retirement savings deducted from our check, which further reduces our take-home pay. The equation looks like this:

(Total pay) - (Federal income tax / Social Security / Medicare / State & Local Taxes / Retirement Savings = Net pay (take-home pay)

Technically, contributing to a retirement savings plan and having that amount deducted from our pay is optional, but it's not really optional because we absolutely need to do this. If our employer has a 401k program, we need to save up to the company match! The other deductions aren't optional and will be deducted from our paycheck each pay period. What's left over is what we'll have to pay our bills and further save.

Federal and State/Local Taxes

We've already discussed how US federal taxes work and that we're taxed based on our income and where that falls into each income tax bracket. Again, in our progressive system, the tax percentage goes higher as we make more income and progress up the brackets. Typically, our employer will automatically deduct our federal taxes from each pay period. At the end of each year, our employer will give us what's called a W-2 form. This document shows us how much we've earned for the year and how much our employer subtracted for the year for federal taxes, state and/or city taxes (if applicable), retirement savings, Social Security and Medicare.

Aside from federal taxes, some states and cities have state and city (local) taxes. Not all states have income tax—for example, Florida and Texas do not. Other states have high state income taxes, like New York, New Jersey, and Connecticut. State and local taxes pay for things like schools and teacher salaries. They pay for city parks and roads, and they also pay for state and local governments. Many states that have high state income taxes have small counties and cities, each with their own mayor and chief of police. States with high taxes also often have state pensions that add a great deal of debt to the state's balance sheet and require taxes to pay pensioners.

An aside: I should add that a state job is often a stable career that typically has a good retirement package, including a pension. The annual pay isn't usually as high as it would be in the public sector, but because state employees have higher job security and good medical and retirement programs, it can certainly be a good life. This is a good example of risk and reward: while a career in the private sector can be high-paying, there's always a risk that we will be let go at any moment, especially if we're not one of the best at what we do. (This is why it's important to become an expert at what we do.) On the other hand, public sector jobs—police, teachers, state offices, military, etc.—carry less risk and typically lower annual compensation, but that security can last all the way through our career and come with a decent retirement package that often includes medical in retirement (which is huge). Public sector jobs are great, but you'll also need to enjoy the role because you really need to stay with the public employer until retirement in order to really maximize the benefits of public sector jobs. Some public sector jobs (like teaching) can reduce your student loan debt as well. It's very easy to go online and find out more about the requirements and roles that "forgive" (i.e., erase) student loan debt.

Social Security and Medicare Taxes

After federal and state/local taxes are paid, then we have Social Security tax deducted from our pay. Social Security is a program run by the Social Security Administration. It's a payroll tax that's deducted; the deduction is then added to a pool of funds that makes monthly payments to retirees. We can start collecting Social Security at the minimum retirement age, or we can wait to start collecting our benefits. The longer we wait to collect from the time we're eligible (easily found online by searching for "minimum Social Security age"), the more we'll get each year. We get more if we wait to start collecting because:

Our life expectancy will be less by then—if we start taking

Social Security at age 70, we might only have another 10 or 15 years to collect it, but if we had started at the eligible age of 62, we would have already taken 8 years of payments by age 70.

1. During those 8 years, our Social Security value will have continued to grow, so we will have earned the extra amount each month by waiting.

After federal, state/local, and Social Security deductions, we have Medicare deductions. Medicare is a federally-run medical insurance program that covers a number of people who might struggle with healthcare costs and who have limited options to obtain insurance through employment. This includes, but isn't limited to, the elderly and persons with disabilities. Medicare is a popular program with the general population because it's thought of as a safety net for people who need medical assistance.

Health Premiums and Retirement Savings Contributions

Those are likely the deductions that most of us will see in our paychecks from our employers. After paying federal, state/local, Social Security and Medicare taxes, we'll need to pay our health insurance premiums and retirement savings contributions. (Again, we should save at least up to the company match.) Having health insurance is obviously important. Younger people typically choose a plan with a high deductible, meaning they pay more when they go to a medical facility. These plans have a low premium cost each pay cycle. If we have a family or have a medical condition, then we might opt for a low-deductible and higher-cost premium plan. This means it's less expensive to visit a doctor, but the amount deducted from our pay is going to be higher.

The deductible is the amount we have to pay up front on an "out-of-pocket" basis. Once we've paid that amount, then the insurance company pays the rest for the year. For example, we might have a $1,000 deductible. This means that if we need medical attention, the first $1,000 is our responsibility to pay (out of our pocket). The insurance company pays for bills over and above $1,000. The deductible usually resets on January 1st. We'll need to pay the first $1,000 out of pocket each year, but then once we've hit that $1,000 during that year, we've met our annual deductible. We should study the plans our employer provides and see which program makes the most sense for our individual situations.

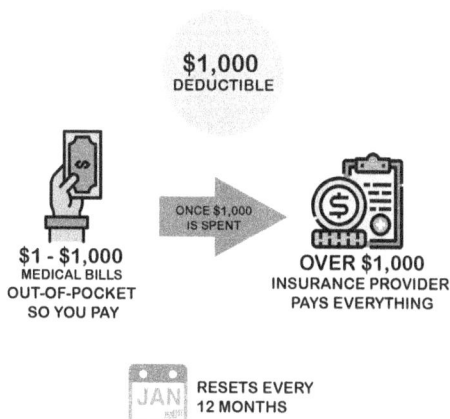

$1,000
DEDUCTIBLE

$1 - $1,000
MEDICAL BILLS
OUT-OF-POCKET
SO YOU PAY

ONCE $1,000
IS SPENT

OVER $1,000
INSURANCE PROVIDER
PAYS EVERYTHING

JAN
RESETS EVERY
12 MONTHS

Many employers offer health insurance, but some don't. (And obviously, if we're self-employed, we won't be offered health insurance—instead, we need to find our own.) We can sign up for a policy once we start working for our employer or during "open enrollment," which is a window of time once a year that allows employees to enter or exit from the employer's healthcare plan. If we're healthy, then maybe we only get the minimum plan, but we do need some form of health insurance as a safety net should something bad happen.

Having an unfortunate health event occur while being un-insured can quite literally financially ruin a person. Uninsured people can face tens of thousands of dollars in healthcare debt if they need substantial medical attention. Hospitals and doctors can and often do charge uninsured patients full prices, which are often much higher than the negotiated pricing that insurance companies have put in place with the same hospitals and doctors. If our employer doesn't offer health insurance, then we can look into the US government's healthcare exchange program. The program offers a variety of healthcare plans that come with government tax credits based on one's income level; these credits lower the cost of individual plans. Visit www.healthcare.gov to find out more about these plans.

We talked about contributions to our 401k plans earlier in the guide. To recap, our employer will likely have a retirement planning option called a 401k. They'll make a contribution to our 401k savings that is typically between 2% and 4% of our pay. They only match the percentage that we personally contribute, so we want to make sure we contribute up to the "company match" so that we maximize the amount of free money we're getting. That's what it is: money on the table that we must take. Our HR person or our manager will be able to quickly give us more information about these plans. Contributions are also made on a pre-tax basis, so our taxable income is reduced by the amount we contribute annually to our 401k. That makes the contributions worth even more!

Although all of these payroll deductions seem high, the reality is that the market has largely baked these costs into our total pay. Just about everybody has these deductions taken out of their checks, so everyone's ratio of take-home pay to total pay is kind of the same. That means prices in the economy are already priced for our net income (take-home pay).

But while this kind of active income through an employer has a number of deductions, income from passive sources (capital gains, dividends, rental property income, etc.) are only subject to federal and state income taxes. Active income from an employer is sometimes referred to as "W-2" income because that's the tax form that employees receive from their employer.

STARTING A BUSINESS

Starting a business can be one of the most exciting things we can do in our professional careers! Being a business owner enables us to be our own boss and not have to depend on others to maintain the lifestyle we want to live. That said, it's important to go into the business with our eyes wide open and to anticipate the challenges that almost all businesses face. The first reality is that most businesses lose money as they get started. Why? Because it takes money to ramp up production of a product or service, and often times there isn't revenue (sales) coming in to pay for the initial expenses. It takes time to educate our market about what value we bring and how we can enrich their lives. The core of any business should be to provide a service or product that makes people's day-to-day lives easier or that solves a problem in our customers' lives. Companies that don't clearly add value or aren't competitive in their field will struggle to keep their business running.

Starting a business doesn't have to be complicated—it can be broken down into a few basic steps and components. First of all, we want to think about the product or service we're offering and define why we want to start the business. The "why" should consider the value the company brings to the market and its customers. Why do we think the business will succeed? Why do customers need our product or service? Why are we interested in offering it? We will then need to develop a business plan that includes market research on customers and other companies offering the same or similar services. The next step is to develop a financial plan by forecasting the business profit/loss each month and determining how much capital (money) we'll need to open and then maintain the business until it becomes profitable. We'll also want to think about the right legal structure so that we can keep our own personal assets protected from any unforeseen litigation (lawsuits) against the business. Lastly, we'll register the business with the right authorities and develop the governing legal documents that are required by the state authorities and the IRS.

This all might sound daunting, but it's not if we break it down step by step and if we develop a team of resources who can help start and maintain the business. Having a team gives perspectives that we might not otherwise have if we're relying only on ourselves. We can't see the full picture when we're in the frame—we need help from others who are standing outside and can help us see the full picture. When we're working really hard on something, we can lose sight of the broader vision. Let's allow people who are removed from the process to provide their perspectives! That can help us refocus on what we want the end picture to look like.

Defining why we want to open the business will help us address whether we have a solution that meets a client's needs or if we're just starting the business because we want to fulfill an internal need. I know that sounds weird, but many new business owners don't fully appreciate the importance of focusing on their customers. The initial step of starting a business shouldn't be purely personal—it should be fact-based and focused on how clients will value what we produce/offer. This initial step includes an assessment of the target audience and how we're going to reach those potential clients.

How will we connect with clients and make both an emotional and a practical connection? By "emotional connection," I mean, how will our customers feel about doing business with us? If we can solve a need and the customer feels good about engaging with us, then our chances of success go up dramatically. It could be as simple as the customer walking away feeling that it was a smooth transaction. As for the practical solution part of the question, that addresses how effective our solution will be at solving our customers' needs or wants.

The answers to these questions change based on the business. If we're opening a business to house our real estate investments, then the emotional connection might be the physical condition of the home and the extent to which it is aligned with the neighborhood in terms of upgrades—tenants can get emotionally connected to a clean, well-maintained, safe house. In this example, the practical aspect could be whether the home is in a good school district or whether it addresses the needs of the target tenant, like whether it's a three-bedroom versus a studio apartment.

Creating a Business Plan

The next step is to develop our business plan. A business plan can be as extensive as we want it to be and can include information on demographics, financing needs, sources of income, and financial planning. If we're manufacturing a product, then the plan should include information about how we're going to actually produce our product or service. What are the costs and start-up efforts? We would also want to outline the channels we'll be using to connect with our customers. Many online guides are available that will walk us through various business plan templates.

A comprehensive business plan should assess the number of people in our target demographic—these people quantify the potential size of our customer base. The plan should also assess how we're going to differentiate ourselves from others in the market who provide the same or similar product/service. What happens if a competitor comes in and competes with us by cutting their prices? How will we drive customers to our product/service?

We'll also want to develop a marketing plan. That means simply identifying how we're going to either remind or educate customers about our business. Marketing can be online campaigns, print ads, promotional products, or using online storefronts like Amazon and Etsy. We can assess the buying patterns of our target audience and think about where they might go to find our product. If we're renting out a property as a product, marketing can be through online rental portals or by using a property manager to market our real estate investment.

Considering the Financial Feasibility of a Business

After we've assessed the market, developed a plan to engage clients, and thought through how we're going to compete against others in the space, then it's time to consider the financial feasibility of our business. I'd argue that this should be at the very top of our list of priorities—after all, our business won't be around long unless it's financially sustainable! Forecasting our company's revenues and costs will allow us to understand the profitability or the losses we can expect in the future. We'll want to start by forecasting monthly sales volumes (monthly revenue). This could be collecting monthly rent(s) on our real estate or forecasting how many products we'll sell each month. We need to remember to ramp up our business forecast by being conservative during the initial months as we market to new customers and grow the business.

Once we've forecasted our revenues (sales), we'll want to think about the costs related to running our business. Just as we talked about our personal costs in the Understanding Expenses section, business costs can be broken down into fixed costs and variable costs. Fixed costs are costs that don't change as we sell our product. If we're producing a physical product, that would be the lease on the real estate we've rented where we manufacture our product. Fixed costs could be the machinery we purchased to assemble or build our product. Those costs are going to be there regardless of whether we make 1 item or 100 items, and they are the ongoing expenses that will recur even if we don't sell a single item. In real estate, an example of a fixed cost could be our annual taxes or our monthly mortgage payments—those will be there whether we've rented the house out or not. If we're selling a service online, the fixed cost could be the monthly cost of maintaining our website.

Our variable costs, on the other hand, go up and down based on our sales volume. A good example would be the material costs of making our product or the labor required to build our product. For a real estate business, the variable costs might be the property management fee that gets paid only if we have a tenant renting the property. Understanding fixed and variable costs is important, because we can obtain "scale" if our fixed costs are high and our variable costs are low, meaning that the cost of every item we sell goes down as we produce more items. That happens because each new item takes on a piece of the fixed cost. If the machinery we purchased to make the product costs us $100, then if we make 10 items, our cost per item is $10...but if we produce 1,000 items, our cost is only $0.10 per item.

We might find that our fixed and variable costs are too high and that we can't achieve profitability no matter how many products we sell. If that's the case, then the business might not be viable. Part of the financial analysis should include start-up costs as well as our break-even analysis. Start-up costs are pretty straightforward—we'll need to assess all the various expenses required to get our business up and running, including product materials, initial legal fees, a sufficient marketing budget and cash reserves to get us through the time where we're ramping up our business and it's likely losing money.

A helpful tool to use here is the break-even analysis. It's simply the amount of time it takes (typically in months) to pay for our upfront costs and investments. It can take months or quarters or sometimes years to break even, so it's important to accurately forecast our sales and costs and ensure that we have enough liquidity (cash) to sustain our business as it grows. We simply forecast our monthly sales and costs (including start-up costs) and then go out as many months as it takes to earn enough net income to equal all of the costs to that date. Many online tools run break-even models as well as offer tools to map out overall business plans.

Funding the Business

There are a number of ways to fund our business and ensure that we have enough cash to survive. Some entrepreneurs get business loans through the SBA (Small Business Administration), some save their own money, and some rely on friends and family. I strongly caution you about garnering funding from friends and family. Relationships can quickly turn sour when we're dealing with money, so make sure you have a very clear plan in place—preferably in writing—around how you're going to pay back your investors. Online crowdsourcing is increasingly becoming a popular way of finding investors who can make small investments, and accumulating many small investments can lead to having enough money to start your business.

Other topics related to starting a business include the type of corporation we want to start and then registering with the right regulatory and tax authorities. Although we can do the research and do these things ourselves, it's best to get the advice of an attorney once we reach this point. An attorney can help with identifying whether we need an S Corp, C Corp, or LLC structure. The vast majority of us will end up with the LLC—it's the typical structure, it's basic, and it protects us personally from business-related liabilities (risks).

LIFE PRO TIP *We all know about the annual Black Friday shopping day. It's named "Black Friday" because many retailers "run in the red" all year until the holiday season. They lose money until Black Friday, when many companies become profitable for the year due to all the sales that take place on that day. That's when their net sales are "in the black." Being "in the red" means the company is losing money; being "in the black" means the company is making money.*

BUYING A HOUSE

Becoming a homeowner is an exciting step because it allows us to take a long-term view of where we're going to live. It also allows us to build wealth over time. We can make our house our own and paint whatever we want and make any kind of adjustments we want. (Renting, on the other hand, limits our ability to customize and make permanent changes to a home.) The term "homeowner" is really just a perception of ownership, though, because the bank actually owns the home until we've paid off the mortgage.

When we enter the housing market, we'll typically need both a realtor and a mortgage lender. The realtor can help with finding a lender if we don't have one. It's a good idea to become "pre-approved" when we start to look at houses so that both the realtor and the seller know that we're actually able to purchase the home. Getting pre-approved simply means that the bank or lender has assessed our credit and provided an initial letter of approval that we can show to the realtor. We need to get our credit score in shape and make sure there are no errors in our report before we have the bank run their lending process. Our interest rate on our mortgage can vary wildly depending on whether we have good credit or bad credit! That's why we should be proactive and fix credit report errors before we start the home-buying process.

We need to be firm with the realtor as to what we're looking for and the price range that meets our budget. Then we need to *not* look at houses over our budget. Looking at homes that are over our budget will only discourage us and might tempt us to spend more than we should.

Leverage

Most homebuyers take out a mortgage to purchase their home. Most mortgage lenders require 20% down, so if the home costs $100,000, we'll be expected to pay $20,000 up front. A mortgage can be a powerful tool that can enable us to purchase a home with what's referred to as "leverage." Leverage means that if we put 20% down on a $100,000 home ($20,000), then as the home appreciates (i.e., goes up in value each year as real estate often does), we benefit from all the upside and the mortgage lender only gets back their principal.

If we have 20% in equity (meaning we put down $20,000 on a $100,000 home), then we have 5 times the leverage. If we sell the $100,000 home for $125,000 five years after we purchased it, then we get our original $20,000 from our down payment back plus the appreciated value. That means we walk away with $45,000. The bank gets none of the appreciation. They just get paid back the outstanding loan amount.

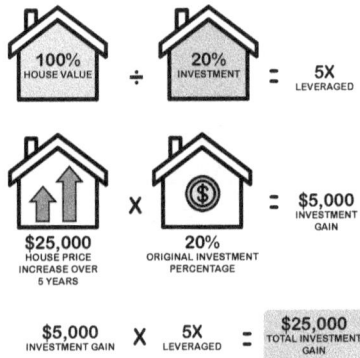

Leverage is an important principle that acts as a multiplier to our investment. We put down 20% of the total 100% of the value of the home, so we're 5 times leveraged (100% / 20% = 5x). Put simply, as the value of an asset goes up, our return on that 20% goes up 5 times. In this example, the price of the house went up $25,000 over 5 years. Because the lender owns the other 80%, we should only see 20% (our original investment percentage) of the $25,000 increase (or $25,000 x 20% = $5,000), but because the mortgage is considered to be leveraged at 5 times, the $5,000 appreciation (which is the $25,000 appreciation x our 20% percentage down payment) goes up by 5 times, which is the $25,000 total appreciation. So we see all the appreciation, and the lender sees none. This goes the other way, too, though. If the house depreciates, then we absorb all of the downside, and the lender still requires that we pay the full amount of the loan.

Principal & Interest

When we make our monthly mortgage payment, we'll be paying what's referred to as P&I, or principal and interest. For example, let's say we purchase a $100,000 home and put down 20% ($20,000) up front. Our mortgage is then $80,000. We have a good credit score, so our interest rate is, say, 5%. In this example, using these figures, our monthly P&I payments would be around $429 per month.

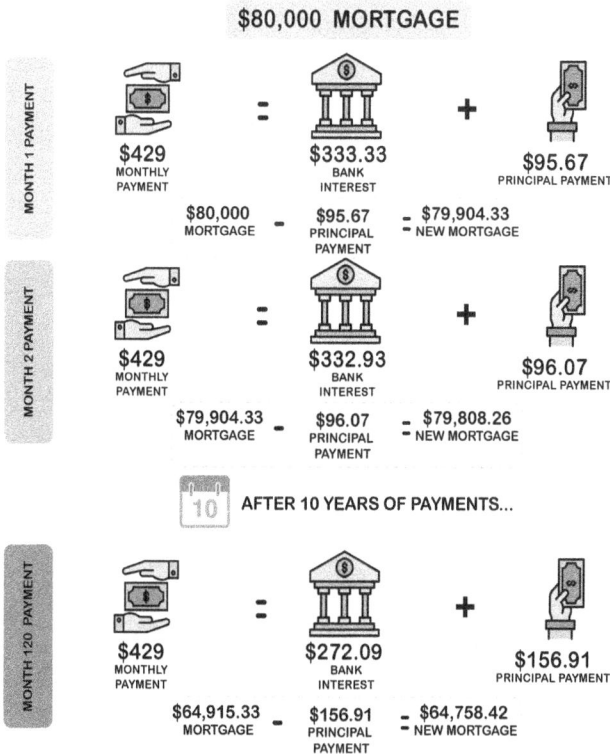

$80,000 MORTGAGE

MONTH 1 PAYMENT

$429
MONTHLY
PAYMENT

=

$333.33
BANK
INTEREST

+

$95.67
PRINCIPAL PAYMENT

$80,000
MORTGAGE

− $95.67
PRINCIPAL
PAYMENT

= $79,904.33
NEW MORTGAGE

MONTH 2 PAYMENT

$429
MONTHLY
PAYMENT

=

$332.93
BANK
INTEREST

+

$96.07
PRINCIPAL PAYMENT

$79,904.33
MORTGAGE

− $96.07
PRINCIPAL
PAYMENT

= $79,808.26
NEW MORTGAGE

10 AFTER 10 YEARS OF PAYMENTS...

MONTH 120 PAYMENT

$429
MONTHLY
PAYMENT

=

$272.09
BANK
INTEREST

+

$156.91
PRINCIPAL PAYMENT

$64,915.33
MORTGAGE

− $156.91
PRINCIPAL
PAYMENT

= $64,758.42
NEW MORTGAGE

Our first month's payment of $429 will be split between interest to the bank ($333.33) and paying down the principal ($95.67). Or put differently, the $95.67 goes towards paying down the $80,000 mortgage. So although our second month's mortgage payment is still the static $429 per month—the payment amount of a fixed mortgage doesn't change for the life of the loan—we just paid $95.67 in principal, so the new principal amount isn't $80,000 but rather $79,904.33 ($80,000 minus $95.97 = $79,904.33). The interest portion of the monthly payment on the new $79,904.33 at 5% is $332.93. That's a little lower than before, and the amount going to the principal goes up a little to $96.07. While this small additional amount going to the principal isn't large initially, it starts to change dramatically. By the time we make a payment 10 years later, when we're making our 120th payment (12 months x 10 years = 120 payments), the amount going to the principal is $156.91 per month. Ten years after that, the monthly principal amount goes up to $272.09 and is really taking a dent out of our principal.

When we consider how this formula works, it becomes more clear why it's so important to try to make an extra payment or two per year, particularly in the early years. If we make a monthly payment amount over our mortgage amount, all the amount over the payment goes directly to the principal. In fact, making just one extra mortgage payment per year will reduce a 30-year mortgage by nearly 5 years because that extra payment goes directly to the principal. That's why we should try to make an extra payment once we've gotten to Step #6 in our financial plan. If we're reading this during a period of time when interest rates are high, then starting earlier (within Step #5) might make sense because we're paying so much in interest for the mortgage alone that it's probably best to make extra contributions to the principal.

Fixed-Rate vs. Variable-Rate Mortgages

Another important factor to understand when financing our home is the two different types of home mortgages: a fixed-rate mortgage and a variable-rate mortgage. A **fixed-rate mortgage** has the same (fixed) rate for the life of the loan. The interest rate is based on how good our credit score is and the rate at which the market is pricing the prime rate. (The prime rate is basically the lowest rate we can get in the market.) The lender looks at our credit profile, our work history, and the taxable income flowing into our household through our employer or other forms of income. The fixed-rate mortgage is good because we have a predictable mortgage payment—the principal and interest are "fixed."

The other form of mortgage is a **variable-rate mortgage**. These were quite popular in the mid-2000s when the US went through the housing bubble and eventual housing crisis. Many people took out variable-rate mortgages because they typically have a lower "teaser" interest rate for the first 3 to 7 years. During that time frame, the rate is fixed. After the initial fixed period ends, however, the rate goes up to the market rate.

In the midst of the housing crisis, people took out variable mortgages with the expectation that they would simply refinance once the initial low fixed rate expired. The problem was that after the low fixed period, many people couldn't refinance because either their houses had gone down in value or they didn't qualify under new mortgage lending standards. Their mortgage payment then increased significantly after the initial low fixed rate, and people couldn't afford their monthly payments. People then defaulted on their homes, which added more inventory to the housing market and further reduced the prices of homes on the market. That made it hard for other people to refinance because they were "underwater." Being underwater means we owe more on our house (through our mortgage) than what it's actually worth at the time.

Generally, it's best to have a fixed-rate mortgage and monitor the mortgage market over the span of ownership. If interest rates significantly drop, we can refinance into another fixed mortgage to lower our rate.

Purchasing the Right Amount of House

We don't want to become "house poor" when purchasing our home. This happens when we've purchased a home that is right on the cusp of what we can afford. If we do that, we can't fill the house with things like furniture because all of our money is going toward our mortgage payments. We should find a house that is well within our means.

It's important not to purchase too much house! The initial price of the home is just the beginning. When we make the purchase, the realtor fees are typically borne by the selling party. The realtor fee is 5% to 6% of the sales price. The buyer pays other fees at closing, which typically amount to 2% to 4% of the home's price. This includes things like the application fee, attorney fees, and lender's title insurance, just to name a few. There are a number of costs related to both purchasing and selling a home, so we need to go into the process with our eyes open. We can find plenty more information about these costs if we do a search for "home closing costs."

Aside from the initial purchasing costs and the monthly mortgage payments, we'll have ongoing maintenance costs. Our maintenance costs will vary depending on the age of the home, the weather conditions where the home is located, the number of people living in the house, etc. (The latter will result in more wear and tear on the home.) It's important that we plan for large expenses like replacing the roof and other high-priced maintenance items. For example, if we know the house has 15 years of roof life left, then we should start saving for that expense well in advance so that we have the necessary funds when we need to replace the roof.

All of our housing expenses are part of our household budget, and we need to develop a realistic budget for owning our home. Owning a house is an important way to grow our wealth, but we do need to make sure that we're conservative about how much house we buy. Too many people purchase the largest home that their budget can handle, which is often times more tied to trying to impress others than actually needing the space. The same goes for lifestyle creep through upsizing our homes. We might genuinely need more space, but we should make an effort to try and stay in a house that's well below our means for as long as we can. As our income goes up over time, our mortgage payment stays the same, letting us really add to our savings during our early years...*if* we don't let our housing costs creep.

LIFE PRO TIP *Mortgages are packaged and sold to investors (typically big investors like insurance companies) who want 30-year mortgage payments at a guaranteed income stream over the 30 years. These investors are buying the loans from the mortgage company that provided the loan to the homeowners who took out a mortgage. These are called mortgage-backed securities, and they're a part of the broader Collateralized Debt Obligation (CDO) space. CDOs are used to bundle debt and then are sold at various risk tranches, with good-credit borrowers in one tranche, medium-credit borrowers in another, and high-risk borrowers (those with lower credit scores) in yet another tranche. The risk goes from low (borrowers with strong credit scores) to high (borrowers with poor credit scores), and the more risky the borrowers are, the higher their interest rate is. Interest rates for borrowers—of homes or of cars—go up as their credit scores go down. Investors demand higher returns on their investments in riskier credit (i.e., people with poor credit scores), so that's why we pay more in credit if we don't maintain our credit score. All of this is to say that we need to get smart about our credit scores—it drives a lot of our ability to access loans at a low interest rate.*

HOW TO SELL, A.K.A. ABC –
ALWAYS BE CLOSING

There are very few career paths where the outcome of our success is largely dependent only upon our own ability. One of those is sales. Sales roles often have two types of compensation: an annual salary and a bonus. Many sales roles reward high-producing salespersons by aligning sales productivity (revenue/volume/other typical sales metrics) with the bonus. A bonus is the portion of the total compensation that's variable and dependent upon how well salespeople meet their sales goals. While there might not be a perfect mathematic equation like "total sales x 10%," often times, the company is a meritocracy where high performers can make 100%+ of their salary (the "+" includes a bonus in the amount of the annual salary) or much higher. The bonus can often be even larger than the annual salary.

At the end of the day, a salesperson is successful if they can identify a need, want, or challenge, and then effectively communicate how their product addresses those needs by correctly positioning the benefits to the buyer. If we believe in the product we're selling and are able to develop a rapport with the buyer, then selling is quite easy—after all, we're offering solutions that meet a need. Confidence comes with frequency. The more we make our pitch, the better we become at pitching. Being able to take "No" for an answer and move on to the next opportunity is critical for success.

Inexperienced salespersons often take a "No" personally, but the longer we're in sales, the more we realize that acting like a "No" didn't even happen is what positions us for the next "Yes." If we have a strong grasp of our client's needs and can effectively communicate how the product meets those needs, then it makes the conversation less about convincing the client to buy and more about how our product (or solution) is assisting the overall goals of the buyer.

I've been in sales all my life, but I've never really thought of myself as a salesperson—I've always thought of it as consulting with the goal of learning my client's needs and then connecting the dots to understand how my products meet the needs of the client. If we're doing high-volume sales, it's pulling on the heartstrings of people who have an emotional connection to the charity we're raising funds for or the product we're selling. If we're selling cars, for example, we need to understand what is motivating the person to enter the lot. We need to understand what's most important to them—safety, for example, if the buyer is a family with children, while middle-aged persons might be looking to relive their youth and want something sporty. We need to play into those emotional needs and position the product in the client's mind to be a great match to meet those needs. (Understanding these techniques puts *us* in a much better position when *we* purchase a product! Understand the mind games being played!)

Although these same basic techniques work across the board when selling, selling higher-value products often requires a greater command of the product being sold. Pharmaceutical sales, for example, require a level of expertise about the drug or medical device. High-value sales also come with a longer sales cycle—it can take weeks or months or even years to close a deal. Sales in some sectors, like banking or software, often include sales that range from $100,000 per sale to over $10 million or more per sale. Some of these sales take years to close and require being very engaged and helpful over the months and quarters. Often, we have to solve problems that might not generate revenue until we finally reach an opportunity that moves the needle sales-wise. Being helpful and supportive to clients will eventually lead to an opportunity.

There's also a softer, less quantifiable aspect of sales, and that is building rapport with our client. This can take the form of making small talk with the customer or inviting the customer out to lunch or dinner. There's truth to the adage that the buyer isn't just purchasing the product—they're also buying into us. People want to do business with people they like and feel comfortable with. This is why common sales techniques include emulating some of the characteristics of the person we're selling to. (People generally love themselves and find joy in things like hearing their name during a sales pitch.) Dressing the part is also critical—we usually can't go wrong by keeping a clean and professional appearance no matter what we're selling. I used to wear a shirt and tie when I was doing phone sales during my college years because it put me in the right frame of mind. Our clients can hear our confidence and won't feel comfortable purchasing from us unless they feel like we know what we're talking about.

We should try to get in the mind of our customer and ask ourselves what we'd need to hear or better understand in order to buy. Effective salespersons might modify their voice inflection and make minor adjustments to mirror the person they're assisting. People feel a sense of comfort when they're dealing with someone similar to themselves. These types of tactics work well when we have short engagements with clients, such as phone sales or one-time episodic sales. We wouldn't want to use these techniques in instances where the sale results in a long-term relationship (like in pharma sales or software sales or the like), but for quick sales, there's a huge benefit to learning how to use these mirroring skills because they allow us to quickly develop a level of trust with the client and establish confidence in how the client views our credibility.

Quick sales require a great first impression. We need to then build upon that by finding common ground (mirroring) and not being afraid to ask for the sale. We should assume the client's going to say "Yes" every time we make a pitch because the client will quickly notice if we're not enthusiastic about our pitch or if we sound anything less than optimistic in our delivery. We should use phases that assume the sale will happen, like "This is how it works," and "We're going to do XYZ." We talk about how the solution will work to solve the client's problem, and we make the sales process as easy as possible in the client's mind.

All that said, we can't ever lie! Salespersons who lie aren't salespersons—they're liars. We can, though, position the sale in the person's mind as being a foregone conclusion—in a truthful way—and lay out the next steps in a way that's easy to understand. We can take any concerns out of the client's mind by educating them. People often get nervous or uncomfortable when they don't understand something, and a salesperson's role is to get the buyer to understand how the solution meets their needs.

Different sales situations will require different skill sets and client engagement tactics. Lower-priced sales are typically a volume play where the margins are thin, so selling in large volume is key. Higher-valued sales typically take longer to close and require the salesperson to be patient yet attentive. There's a fine line between being responsive/helpful and being annoying. Being annoying is the quickest way to lose a potential sale and customer. We should read our client's behavior! If they say it's not a priority right now, then fine—we won't continue to pester them. Rather, we'll take the position that we understand priorities evolve over time and that we'll follow up in the next month or quarter.

In the meantime, we can find helpful ways to add value outside of the sale we're looking to make. That can include sending updates on specific market topics, occasionally inviting the client to lunch/dinner or maybe to a sports event, or to play a round of golf. But we shouldn't pitch during these interactions! The client needs to feel as though the time together is time we *want* to spend together and not just another setting to get the chance to sell something. I don't typically make a pitch in social settings unless the client makes the first move. Instead, I use the time to develop rapport and a sense of friendship (i.e., a mutual level of respect). Both will go a long way to building equity for down the road when the time for pitching is more appropriate. It's always helpful in sales to genuinely take an interest in others.

When we're in sales, it also helps to think of ourselves as relationship managers. Relationship managers manage the dialog between the client and the business. They have the long game in mind and understand that every little positive interaction will be stored away for a later date. But all of that stored-away "equity" is quickly lost if we let the relationship take a negative tone, so we need to do our best to get involved in issues and be the person who stays on top of the problem until it's solved.

LIFE PRO TIP *Eventually, we'll find ourselves in a situation where there's a problem with a client. Maybe we or someone on the team dropped the ball. Maybe there was a technology issue with the solution. When faced with client issues, it's important that we professionally address the situation in a holistic manner. We need to think of solving client problems by answering these questions: "What happened?" "How did it happen?" "What did we do to fix it?" and "What did we do or put in place to ensure it never happens again?" When addressing an issue with a client, we should always frame the problem within this context and have solid answers to these questions.*

HOW TO NEGOTIATE

Negotiating should not be viewed as a way to win or take advantage of a situation or person. Real negotiating is based on each side understanding the value they bring and assessing how aggressively they can negotiate based on how strong their hand is. If we're selling something that's of very high value or is rare, then we obviously have a great deal of power. If that rare item has very few buyers because it might be related to a very unique hobby, for example, then our negotiating starting point might not be as strong.

We have to put ourselves in the mind of the other party—the buyer or the seller—and understand what they want to accomplish or what their goal is. If we're negotiating our salary, for example, we should understand how our employer is evaluating us and then we should lay out the value we bring to the organization by focusing on the performance metrics that are being evaluated. Through those metrics, our employer is assessing whether we bring enough unique value to the role and whether our performance is high enough to justify the increase in pay.

The best negotiation is a "win-win" result where all parties feel they've had a good outcome and have largely met the goals they had going into the negotiation. We're going to use negotiating skills throughout our lives, including in many instances where we might not even think we're negotiating. After all, we're going to have to use some form of negotiating *any* time we're seeking the help or assistance of another person/party to fulfill one of our goals or objectives. Let's think about the most common instances where we're going to need to negotiate: when buying something, when selling something, or when negotiating a desired outcome, like an increase in salary.

Buying and Selling Things

When it comes to buying and selling, if we only value the economic outcome and there really won't be any emotional or ongoing tie with our counterparty after the negotiation, then statistically, we're better off making the first offer. This applies when an item is being sold and all parties will walk away afterward, never to engage again. Buying a car or home or something off a website are good examples of this. The first offer allows us to anchor the outcome in our favor because we can set a reasonably low bar. That said, we don't want to offend the seller or buyer with a lowball offer that blows up the negotiation. The other party needs to feel that the offer is serious and not a waste of their time. We should also understand that the seller likely has some emotional connection with the item, so we want to show them that we value the item (car, home, etc.) and appreciate the sentimental value the item might have for the seller. When we only care about the monetary outcome, we need to take all emotion out of the process. People get attached to things very quickly and lose negotiating power when there's an emotional connection.

If we're selling, there's a risk to accepting a low offer without negotiating, namely that it sends the wrong message to the buyer. The buyer might think that the item isn't even worth the new, low offer because the seller quickly accepted it. If we're the seller and we're happy with a low ball offer, we should take a little time to think about that price and maybe even go back with a number that's marginally higher than the initial offer. If we just take an offer that's much lower than our original asking price, we can send the wrong message and might scare the buyer away. Also, if we're the seller, it can be helpful to get the buyer to have an emotional connection to what we're selling. We can listen or look for clues from the other party that might give insight as to what soft (intangible) values are involved with the item being negotiated. Whatever those values are, we should be adding to their emotional connection so that the buyer feels they need or want the item for reasons beyond just the price.

Before we enter into the negotiation, we should think about the pressure points for all parties. Maybe the real estate investment we're looking at is an empty house that's been vacant for months. In that case, the seller is likely motivated to sell. Think about the seller's circumstances and what variables play a role in the seller considering a lower price. What goal can we let the seller achieve over and above the sales price? Maybe that same house is behind in taxes, and we can offer to pay off the delinquent balances as a part of the deal, which helps the seller avoid foreclosure. Can we pay with either cash or some other form of payment that potentially lowers the seller's selling costs? If we're in a hot seller's market, we can consider "sweeteners" that might make our offer more appealing, like purchasing a real estate investment without an inspection.

Another strategy is to add deadlines to our offer. This applies pressure for the buyer or seller to feel a sense of urgency. It also makes the other party feel like we have other options to consider. Psychologically, this pushes the person we're negotiating with to be more open-minded about our offer.

Negotiating Salaries

Up to this point, we've largely discussed negotiating an item that's being sold or purchased, but negotiating our salary is also a very important skill. The key to salary negotiations is to focus on how we're going to pay for ourselves and how the increase in salary is marginal compared to the value we're adding.

Negotiating at Our Current Job

Most companies have what's referred to as "cost centers" or "profit centers." If we're a part of a cost center, our role is likely to support the manufacturing of the product or service. That makes us a cost of doing business. We might be involved with customer service, IT, logistics, accounting, engineering design, etc. If we do have a cost center role, it's important to focus on ways in which we can help save the company money or possibly even add to the company's revenue. When negotiating a cost center role, we should focus on how efficient we can be and how our past experience has enabled us to process more work compared to others who have the role. If we're already employed by the company, we can focus on things we've already done to drive down costs.

No company is going to pay us more if we haven't demonstrated that we are adding more marginal value than what we're getting paid for. Feeling entitled to a raise just because we've been with the same company for 2 or 5 or 10 years isn't how we should see salary increases or advancement with our employer. We have to be someone whom our immediate boss values; if we were to leave the company, we would be leaving our boss in a difficult situation. It's a mistake to think that a company is keeping us around just because they like us—we have to add enough value to earn our salary.

Introducing new ideas that save the company money or improve efficiency is how we earn a salary increase. This is what positions us to be able to realistically negotiate a higher fixed salary or hourly rate. We must be able to quantify the value we bring and show that bringing in someone else to do our job would cost the company more *and* result in a less efficient or value-added employee. At the end of the day, we get paid for the skill that differentiates us. It's a tough reality, but if we don't add value over and above what someone else is adding, then we're going to be paid very little at most companies. After all, if we're easily replaceable, why should a company pay us more? It's harsh, but it's simply the way the system works. Companies pay us so that we continue to come to the job. If they can swap us out with ease, then the role just isn't going to pay much. The sooner we understand this, the sooner we're on track to career advancement.

Now, if we're in a profit center role, we're likely in sales or in a role that directly drives the selling process. Negotiating a salary increase in a profit center role is almost entirely based on how productive we are and how we can causally relate our efforts to "top-line revenue." Top-line revenue is simply another way of saying "total sales." If we've shown continued growth in our contribution to the firm's sales, then it will be much easier and more natural for us to negotiate. Also, if we're in a sales role, the company may want to keep us around because we're the "face of the company." Having relationships with our employer's customers carries a lot of value—our employer will typically pay us to remain and keep the customer happy and committed. Customers don't like change, so we have more power in our salary negotiations if we play a role in the relationships that the company has with its customers.

We can use the value of our relationships with customers (this could simply be our ability to connect with others) and our quantifiable sales contributions as the centerpiece for our negotiations. Seeing as unsuccessful salary negotiations are typically based on using entitlement as a reason for an increase in pay, we should avoid saying that we've been around long enough and therefore deserve an increase. Let's also avoid comparing our compensation with what others are getting, like saying we heard that our colleague gets paid X amount and we want a raise. That's another angle that doesn't typically end well. Instead, we can compare our efficiency to others and outline why we should be paid more. Simply put, we produce more! We can look at the metrics we're measured against and show that we perform at a higher level than our peers and hence deserve to be rewarded at a higher rate.

Negotiating for a New Job/Role

We've talked about negotiating a salary when we are already employed. Now let's discuss negotiating a salary for a new job or role. Our negotiating position will differ depending on whether we're already employed, whether our new job will be more demanding than the one we currently have (meaning it will be more stressful and/or require more hours per week) and whether the offer we've received is below, at, or above the market rate. Also, negotiating a new job isn't just about salary. We should also consider negotiating our title, vacation days, relocation expenses (if applicable), etc. A word of caution about titles: what we're getting paid is often more important than what our title is. We can't put food on the table or purchase our next investment property with an inflated title but subpar compensation.

Before we start to negotiate our salary for a new job, we need to do our research as to how the role is valued in the market and think about how our contributions will put us above the competition. Also, we should never negotiate a salary unless we've been given an offer—meaning, we won't talk about money until we've sold the company on hiring us. The salary component of our job will certainly be discussed, but most employers want to know if we're the right fit for the role first and *then* talk money.

We also want the process to play out so that we know the company is the right fit for us. Even though the company is interviewing us, we're also interviewing the company! We shouldn't be overconfident, but we should ask questions about important aspects we're looking for with our employer, like what the corporate culture is like and how success is measured for the role we're interviewing for. Negotiating a salary becomes much easier once we've gone through the interview process and the company knows we're the right person—we shouldn't get things offtrack by discussing our salary before the company has fully bought into what we bring to the table.

When asked about our salary expectations, it's fair to state that we're flexible and that we're looking for the right opportunity. If further pressed, we can ask the employer what the compensation range is and reply with a number that makes it worthwhile to leave our current role and start fresh with a new company. A decent rule of thumb is to expect a 10% to 20% increase in salary because of the effort required to start over at a different company. That said, if we're not currently employed, we might not want to be as aggressive with the salary negotiation process because we simply need a role. We don't want to act desperate—we don't want the company to think that we're not in demand—but we also might not want to pay hardball once given a reasonable offer.

The bottom line for negotiating a salary is that we're compensated for the value we bring to a company. The cost of every job in a company is included in their future forecasts for revenues and expenses. If we can outline how we can either add more revenue or help reduce expenses, then we become more valuable than what was forecasted, and that increase in revenue or decrease in expenses can help pay for our proposed salary increase. We shouldn't undersell ourselves and take a role that doesn't pay us the value we offer, but we should also be aware of how other companies pay for the same role. We should also not be greedy. It's much easier to start with a company at a reasonable starting pay, use our first year or two to show what value we bring, and *then* negotiate up once the company sees what we can do for them.

Working Our Way Up

There's also an element of wanting to get our foot in the door. If we want to be in marketing or the music business or banking and we don't have any connections and we didn't join some graduate program out of college, then we'll need to start low and prove ourselves. We can work our way up by building internal relationships and doing more than our peers are doing. In the Building a Brand at Work section, we talked about the fact that people who advance in a company have two skills: 1) they can get people to like them, and 2) they have a full understanding of the expectations of the role and can exceed employer expectations. It might take years before we start to see traction—that's not uncommon. But if we continue to stand out from the crowd and develop internal relationships, then we will gradually move up.

We're also building our résumé while we're working our way up. In other words, we increasingly have experience on the job. That will make applying to work at other companies a much more productive process should our current employer not help our career progress. I'll also add that although staying with the same company for a long time has its benefits (such as familiarity and close relationships with colleagues), it often times comes with a big downside, namely that our salary will likely be lower than if we moved a couple of times throughout our career. That's because while our employer isn't likely going to give us a 10% to 20% raise in a given year, getting that increase is common when we move to another employer. If we're lucky, we might get a 2% to 3% raise each year to match the increased cost of living due to inflation. More substantial increases often come when we move to another company. Our salary can really accelerate if we get a couple of 10% to 20% bumps in pay! But unfortunately, that comes along with transitioning to another employer.

LIFE PRO TIP *The information in our résumé should be laid out the same way that we outline the value we've added with past employers when we negotiate with potential new employers—we can include numbers that detail how we performed, like key performance metrics. If we had value-added suggestions that either generated revenue or saved our employer costs, we should include those examples (with numbers) in our résumé. We should lay out clear examples of how we can contribute to our next employer's bottom line (net income).*

We might also hear a résumé referred to as a "CV," or curriculum vitae. It's Latin for "course of life," and it's just a fancy way of saying résumé. (This is also more commonly used by companies headquartered outside of the US.) We don't need to be caught off guard if we see the term CV.

HOW MUCH MONEY DO I NEED TO RETIRE?

Having a sense of what it takes to retire is something that might not be top of mind in our younger years, but that's exactly the time when it's the most important to invest. It's critical to open the various retirement (nontaxable) accounts and brokerage accounts (taxable accounts) we'll need to maximize our retirement efforts. The power of compound interest is a tool that we have to appreciate and understand.

As a point of reference, if we invest $5,000 per year between the ages of 25 and 35 (for just 10 years early in life), we'd have over $600,000 saved by the time we're 65 years old. If we started 10 years later (at age 35) and started investing $5,000 per year and kept investing $5,000 per year for the next 30 years (so from age 35 to 65), we'd "only" have $540,000. Thanks to the power of compounding interest over time, we end up with $60,000 more at age 65 by only investing $5,000 from age 25 to 35 (10 years) versus investing $5,000 for 30 years. But it's never too late to start investing in our future! Although investing at a young age really makes our money work for us and is the best time to start saving, the second-best time to start saving and investing is *right now*.

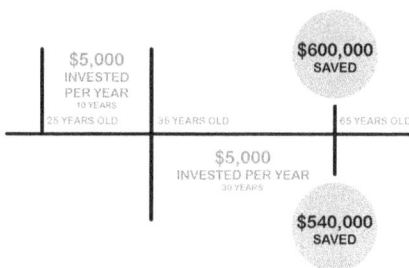

$5,000
INVESTED
PER YEAR
10 YEARS
25 YEARS OLD   35 YEARS OLD   65 YEARS OLD

$600,000
SAVED

$5,000
INVESTED PER YEAR
30 YEARS

$540,000
SAVED

Back to the retirement question. Most people don't really know how to think about retirement savings, partially because the financial industry does a great job of making things sound complicated. One of the reasons for this is to confuse consumers and have them purchase investments that are geared towards retirement savings but have high costs/fees that benefit the financial institution over time. A good example of this is an annuity policy. Annuities are financial instruments that have us contribute to the annuity over, say, 20 or 30 years. They then have a guaranteed monthly payout (or income to us) at retirement. These plans are very expensive, and often times simply investing the same amount each month into a low-cost index fund (FSKAX, for example) will result in more savings at age 65 because we don't have the high transaction costs (fees) associated with annuities. Also, annuities are often commission-based, which means the representative from the financial institution makes a commission on selling us the annuity. Some would argue there is a conflict of interest here. It's not a great idea to take financial advice from someone who stands to make money off of their investment recommendations.

I typically recommend going to a fee-based financial advisor, one who charges an upfront set fee and then provides financial guidance. This kind of advisor does not benefit from the financial guidance they provide. Because having a fee-based advisor removes any conflict of interest, we have less risk of being put into an investment vehicle that doesn't have our best interests in mind and may instead be putting the financial institution's interests ahead of ours. We want only fee-based financial advisors, *not* commission-based.

The math for retiring is quite easy—all we need to do is develop a budget for retirement and then have enough savings to meet the needs of our budget. This is where having multiple income streams in retirement is important. Many people will retire and rely only on Social Security to fund their retirement. Although people can get by on only Social Security, it's not a lifestyle that will afford us a budget that allows for travel or typical retirement hobbies. Yes, we might be able to pay for food and hopefully housing if we're still paying a mortgage (better yet, hopefully we're living in a home that's paid off), but it's simply not the lifestyle we would likely want to live during our elder years. Saving for retirement early in life is the key to having a retirement we can enjoy.

Let's say we have our retirement budget in mind. For illustrative purposes, we'll need $75,000 per year to live the lifestyle we wish to live. As we discussed in the Financial Independence

| $75,000 | $18,000 | $57,000 |
| LIFESTYLE COSTS PER YEAR | YEARLY SOCIAL SECURITY PAYMENT | LIFESTYLE COSTS SELF-FUND |

| $57,000 | X 25 | $1,425,000 |
| LIFESTYLE COSTS SELF-FUNDED | | COMFORTABLY RETIRE |

section, we'll need to have enough money saved to allow us to withdraw 4% of our net worth that equals that $75,000 in expenses. If we aren't pursuing early retirement, we can deduct our Social Security income from the $75,000. What's left is what needs to be funded. Let's assume we're forecasted to earn $18,000 per year, which is the average Social Security payment. We'll then need to self-fund $57,000 ($75,000 minus $18,000 = $57,000). Going back to the Financial Independence section, we'll need to have 25 times that amount (for a 4% safe withdrawal rate) or $1,425,000 to comfortably retire and have our money last us for another 25 to 30 years. If we're in our late 60s or early 70s, maybe we can increase the safe withdrawal rate to 5%, but that still means we need to save over $1 million.

So let's start now! Let's start saving for retirement as soon as we're employed because even though that $1 million-plus amount looks daunting, it's manageable with time and compounding interest. When we have youth on our side, we should take advantage of the two most important factors behind accumulating wealth: time and compounding interest.

In Conclusion

E ven after you've read about these topics, you likely still have a lot of questions and ideas. This book should be thought of as the first step down a path of continued learning. We've spent time discussing some of the most important principles in life, but we must continue to learn about these themes in order to truly understand them and be able to put them to use.

I hope this book has opened your mind to thinking differently about your future, to knowing that you *do* have control of your life and can create the path you want. That you're not a byproduct of your past but that, rather, you can create your own environment and the life you want to live. It will take time, though. I was not patient when I was first out of school—I felt like I was always behind. You might feel the same way. I like to think of that feeling as being the drive we need to keep us motivated, but at the same time, we can't let that drive overshadow the small successes we achieve each day or week or month.

Now it's time to step back and think about your goals in life. Write down those goals so that they're clear and quantifiable, then periodically review them and track your progress. Think about your financial goals in particular and review the 7 steps outlined in the Personal Finance section. Start with Step #1 and put that into action, then move to Step #2, and so on. Simply follow the process one step at a time.

Stay motivated! Start thinking about how you'd like to continue to feed yourself with motivational messages. Some people enjoy reading books like *Think and Grow Rich* and *The Power of Positive Thinking*. (Also, look into books by Les Brown and Bob

Proctor.) I prefer the spoken word, so for me, YouTube videos work very well. Search for "motivational speeches," and you'll find hours of content.

Whatever your preferred method, you simply must continue to stay motivated in order to keep up the momentum. Your brain will revert back to its old ways of negative self-talk because that's how we've been conditioned. Just reading this book one time will not reverse what's been ingrained into your psyche. Yes, this book does provide a blueprint as to how you can reprogram your mind (and I've done my best to point out the unproductive aspects of the way all of us sometimes think), but recognizing these variables is just the first step to learning. I did not realize how important reprogramming was when I graduated from school! Having a positive attitude and a positive mindset is crucial for success. When people ask me how to become successful, the very first thing I tell them is that they have to have the mentality of success.

Lastly, we need to recognize that our journey will take many different paths and that things typically don't play out as we first expected. We need to be able to pivot and learn from one approach so that we can try a different one and get a different result. There's very rarely a straight line from where we are now to where our goals will lead us, and often, things will get harder before they get easier. That's why so few people achieve their life goals—things get hard, and they quit. And we need to remember that more often than not, the decisions we've made up until right now led to where we are right now. Maybe we didn't take school seriously because we didn't have the right influencers in our life. Maybe the people we hung out within our youth led to us getting in trouble. Maybe we had a child at a very young age and we feel we're limited. Maybe we grew up in a house that didn't value education, or we didn't have a role model who emulated any of the topics in this book.

Whatever our situation is, we need to think about the very next step we need to take to get on our journey. We can change our trajectory and start looking at ways to build our skills, whether that's going to college or trade school or learning a skill that will make us stand out. We can overcome any self-imposed roadblocks. We need to make it our priority to push on and keep overcoming challenges. Taking responsibility for where we are right now will give us the confidence that we can control our future. The confidence of knowing that *we* write the book of our own lives, and that book isn't even close to being completed.

Call to Action:

So, we've read the book – now what?

- **PERSONAL FINANCE – GET DISCIPLINED**

  ○ Schedule 1 hour with yourself to start to assess your budget
  ○ Be honest with yourself about your needs and wants
  ○ Assess your income and determine how you can grow your household revenue through developing skills (for career advancement) and / or getting a second job

    • *Drive for a delivery service? Work from home customer service roles?*
    • *Google 'side gig jobs' and start to apply*

- Constructively think about your skills and put together a plan for up-tiering so that you can maximize your time at work (trade school or local college)

  ○ Reexamine and map out the 7 steps and put together your execution plan
  ○ Review your credit cards that have balances and rank from the highest interest rate to lowest interest rate

- Talk to your HR and set up your 401k (ask about the company match)
- Find a brokerage provider (Fidelity / Vanguard / Charles Schwab / Merrill Lynch / etc.), open an investment account (IRA and non-retirement accounts), and deposit $10 to get the plumbing up and running

- **MINDSET FOR SUCCESS**

  - Go to YouTube and look for "motivational speeches" or "motivational videos"
  - Find two more books to start your library – suggest "Think and Grow Rich" by Napoleon Hill and "Rich Dad Poor Dad" by Robert T. Kiyosaki – these are classics
  - Join Reddit forums – suggest 'Financial Independence' / 'Personal Finance' / 'Landlord'
  - Join Facebook groups – suggest 'AP Adulting' / 'Adulting 101 – We Can Do It' / 'FIRE: Financial Independence Retire Early'

- **WE ALL HAVE TO START SOMEWHERE WITH MEASURED STEPS. DON'T PROCRASTINATE AND FORGET WHAT WE'VE DISCUSSED OVER THE COURSE OF THIS BOOK. KEEP LEARNING AND TAKE ACTION! THIS IS YOUR LIFE, AND YOU DESERVE THE VERY BEST!**

About the Author

Establishing his work on a foundation of integrity, John Chadwick is a renowned Finance/Banking Executive, Entrepreneur, and Author who enjoys guiding others toward attaining new levels of financial literacy and fruitful independence. As a Managing Director for a global bank, John holds an extensive 25+ year history involving the intricacies of money/business management, multi-national banking relations, and inspiring healthy mindset shifts beyond standard education, taking pride in leveraging that dynamicity to prove anyone can achieve their own definition of success with the right tools, support, and splashes of motivation.

Based in NYC with his amazing wife, whom he has started several businesses with, John discovered early on the innate value of under-the-surface education, possessing a strong work ethic, and moral compass leadership. Part of that stems from his humble upbringing being raised by a hard-working single mother, and the other from his first-hand experience seeing just how disconnected formal education was at preparing society for real-world success. Upon earning a BA and MA in Business Administration, John spent the next two decades of his life figuring out adulthood, rectifying mistakes and overcoming hurdles that were never brought up in the classroom. But with much perseverance, John soon became a franchise owner, built a real estate holding company, and is a Global Relationship Manager at one of the world's largest financial institutions. Even more, has since blended those versed experiences to help guide all walks of life towards not just attaining the financially balanced futures they deserve but ultimately teaching them how to spearhead the wealth-building game along the way.

In the end, a person either disciplines their finances or their finances discipline them. Because the truth is that there is a secret psychology of money that dives deeper than what traditional education prepares you for where a lack of money is not the problem; it is merely just a symptom of what is going on in your own thoughts - ultimately inspiring John to write 'Advance Placement (AP) Adulting' and finally bridging those prevalent gaps to enable his readers to thrive in every facet of their lives. Overall, there is no denying that it takes a lot of dedication to break the molded narratives revolving around financial literacy and wealth, and sometimes all it takes is connecting with someone who cares about your future trajectories as much as you do to finally recognize and capitalize on that.

From executive banking to authoring void-filling publications, nothing makes John happier than being able to help others achieve their own unique version of success and ultimately excel in the real world. However, when he is not working, you can usually find him snow skiing, traveling internationally, scuba diving, staying active, practicing the art of mindfulness, and above all, spending time with his biggest supporter – his wife.

About The Author

220

Advanced Placement (AP) Adulting

www.ingramcontent.com/pod-product-compliance
Lightning Source LLC
Chambersburg PA
CBHW031849200326
41597CB00012B/341